A Midsummer Night's Dream

Webster's Italian Thesaurus Edition

for ESL, EFL, ELP, TOEFL®, TOEIC®, and AP® Test Preparation

William Shakespeare

ICON CLASSICS

Published by ICON Group International, Inc.
7404 Trade Street
San Diego, CA 92121 USA

www.icongrouponline.com

A Midsummer Night's Dream: Webster's Italian Thesaurus Edition for ESL, EFL, ELP, TOEFL®, TOEIC®, and AP® Test Preparation

This edition published by ICON Classics in 2005
Printed in the United States of America.

ISBN 0-497-90708-9

Contents

PREFACE FROM THE EDITOR 1

PERSONS REPRESENTED 2

ACT I 4

ACT II 20

ACT III 38

ACT IV 68

ACT V 80

GLOSSARY 100

PREFACE FROM THE EDITOR

Webster's paperbacks take advantage of the fact that classics are frequently assigned readings in English courses. By using a running English-to-Italian thesaurus at the bottom of each page, this edition of *A Midsummer Night's Dream* by William Shakespeare was edited for three audiences. The first includes Italian-speaking students enrolled in an English Language Program (ELP), an English as a Foreign Language (EFL) program, an English as a Second Language Program (ESL), or in a TOEFL® or TOEIC® preparation program. The second audience includes English-speaking students enrolled in bilingual education programs or Italian speakers enrolled in English speaking schools. The third audience consists of students who are actively building their vocabularies in Italian in order to take foreign service, translation certification, Advanced Placement® (AP®)[1] or similar examinations. By using the Webster's Italian Thesaurus Edition when assigned for an English course, the reader can enrich their vocabulary in anticipation of an examination in Italian or English.

Webster's edition of this classic is organized to expose the reader to a maximum number of difficult and potentially ambiguous English words. Rare or idiosyncratic words and expressions are given lower priority compared to "difficult, yet commonly used" words. Rather than supply a single translation, many words are translated for a variety of meanings in Italian, allowing readers to better grasp the ambiguity of English, and avoid them using the notes as a pure translation crutch. Having the reader decipher a word's meaning within context serves to improve vocabulary retention and understanding. Each page covers words not already highlighted on previous pages. If a difficult word is not translated on a page, chances are that it has been translated on a previous page. A more complete glossary of translations is supplied at the end of the book; translations are extracted from Webster's Online Dictionary.

Definitions of remaining terms as well as translations can be found at www.websters-online-dictionary.org. Please send suggestions to websters@icongroupbooks.com

The Editor
Webster's Online Dictionary
www.websters-online-dictionary.org

---

[1] TOEFL®, TOEIC®, AP® and Advanced Placement® are trademarks of the Educational Testing Service which has neither reviewed nor endorsed this book. All rights reserved.

PERSONS REPRESENTED

THESEUS, Duke of Athens.

EGEUS, Father to Hermia.

LYSANDER,
DEMETRIUS, } in love with Hermia

PHILOSTRATE, Master of the Revels to Theseus.

QUINCE, the Carpenter.

SNUG, the Joiner.

BOTTOM, the Weaver.

FLUTE, the Bellows-mender.

SNOUT, the Tinker.

STARVELING, the Tailor.

HIPPOLYTA, Queen of the Amazons, bethrothed to Theseus.

HERMIA, **daughter** to Egeus, in love with Lysander.

HELENA, in love with Demetrius.

OBERON, King of the Fairies.

TITANIA, Queen of the Fairies.

PUCK, or Robin Goodfellow, a Fairy.

PEASBLOSSOM,
COBWEB,
MOTH, } fairies
MUSTARDSEED,

Italian

bottom: fondo, basso, carena.
daughter: figlia, figliola, figliuola, la
  figlia.
flute: flauto, scanalatura.
puck: disco.
quince: mela cotogna, cotogna.
snout: muso, sigaretta, grifo, grugno.
snug: accogliente, comodo, raccolto.

PYRAMUS,
THISBE,
WALL,   }   characters in the **interlude** perform'd
MOONSHINE,   by the Clowns
LION

Other FAIRIES **attending** their KING and QUEEN. ATTENDANTS on THESEUS
and HIPPOLYTA.

Italian

attending: visitando, curando,
  assistendo.
interlude: intermezzo, interludio,
  intervallo.

ACT I

SCENE I. **ATHENS**. A ROOM IN THE PALACE OF THESEUS.

[Enter THESEUS, HIPPOLYTA, PHILOSTRATE, and ATTENDANTS.]

THESEUS

Now, **fair** Hippolyta, our **nuptial** hour
Draws on **apace**; four **happy** days **bring** in
Another **moon**; but, oh, methinks, how slow
This old moon **wanes**! she **lingers** my desires,
Like to a step-dame or a dowager,
Long **withering** out a young man's **revenue**.

HIPPOLYTA

Four days will **quickly steep** themselves in nights;
Four nights will quickly **dream** away the time;
And then the moon, like to a **silver** bow
New **bent** in **heaven**, shall **behold** the night
Of our solemnities.

THESEUS

Go, Philostrate,
Stir up the Athenian **youth** to merriments;
Awake the **pert** and **nimble spirit** of mirth;

Italian

apace: di buon passo.
athens: Atene.
behold: guardare.
bent: curvo, piegato.
bring: portare, portiamo, porti, portano, portate, porto, porta.
dream: sogno, sognare.
fair: biondo, fiera, giusto, bazar, correttamente, bello, equo.
happy: felice, contento, lieto, beato.
heaven: cielo, paradiso.
lingers: indugia.

moon: luna, la luna.
nimble: agile.
nuptial: nuziale.
pert: impertinente.
quickly: presto, rapidamente, velocemente.
revenue: reddito, entrata, ricavi.
silver: argento.
spirit: spirito, anima.
steep: ripido, erto, scosceso.
wanes: declina.
withering: avvizzimento, appassendo.

youth: gioventù, giovinezza, adolescenza, giovane.

Turn **melancholy forth** to funerals--
The **pale companion** is not for our **pomp**. --
[Exit PHILOSTRATE.]
Hippolyta, I woo'd **thee** with my sword,
And won **thy** love doing thee injuries;
But I will **wed** thee in another key,
With pomp, with **triumph**, and with revelling.

[Enter EGEUS, HERMIA, LYSANDER, and DEMETRIUS.]

EGEUS

Happy be Theseus, our **renowned duke**!

THESEUS

Thanks, good Egeus: what's the news with thee?

EGEUS

Full of **vexation** come I, with complaint
Against my child, my daughter Hermia.--
Stand forth, Demetrius.--My **noble** lord,
This man hath my **consent** to **marry** her:--
Stand forth, Lysander;--and, my **gracious** duke,
This man hath bewitch'd the **bosom** of my child.
Thou, **thou**, Lysander, thou hast given her rhymes,
And interchang'd love-tokens with my child:
Thou hast by **moonlight** at her window sung,
With **feigning** voice, verses of feigning love;
And stol'n the **impression** of her fantasy
With bracelets of thy hair, **rings**, gawds, conceits,
Knacks, trifles, nosegays, sweetmeats,--messengers
Of strong prevailment in unharden'd youth;--
With **cunning** hast thou filch'd my daughter's heart;
Turned her **obedience**, which is **due** to me,
To **stubborn** harshness.--And, my gracious duke,
Be it so she will not here before your **grace**

Italian

bosom: petto, seno.
companion: compagno, accompagnatore.
consent: consenso, concordare, essere d'accordo, accordo, benestare, assenso, acconsentire.
cunning: astuzia, astuto, furbo.
due: dovuto.
duke: duca.
feigning: fingendo.
forth: avanti.
grace: grazia.

gracious: grazioso.
impression: impressione, impronta.
marry: sposare, sposati, sposatevi, si sposi, si sposate, si sposano, ci sposiamo, mi sposo, maritarsi, ammogliarsi, maritare.
melancholy: malinconia, malinconico.
moonlight: chiaro di luna.
noble: nobile, gentilizio, nobiliare.
obedience: ubbidienza, obbedienza.
pale: pallido, smorto, impallidire.
pomp: pompa, fasto.

renowned: rinomato, famoso.
rings: anelli.
stubborn: ostinato, testardo, cocciuto, caparbio.
thee: te.
thou: tu.
thy: tuo.
triumph: vittoria, trionfo.
vexation: irritazione.
wed: sposarsi, sposare, ci sposiamo, sposati, sposatevi, si sposi, si sposate, mi sposo, si sposano.

Consent to marry with Demetrius,
I **beg** the **ancient privilege** of Athens,--
As she is **mine** I may **dispose** of her:
Which shall be either to this **gentleman**
Or to her death; **according** to our law
Immediately **provided** in that case.

THESEUS

What say you, Hermia? be advis'd, fair maid:
To you your father should be as a god;
One that compos'd your beauties: yea, and one
To **whom** you are but as a form in wax,
By him imprinted, and within his power
To leave the **figure**, or **disfigure** it.
Demetrius is a **worthy** gentleman.

HERMIA

So is Lysander.

THESEUS

                    In himself he is:
But, in this kind, **wanting** your father's voice,
The other must be held the worthier.

HERMIA

I would my father look'd but with my eyes.

THESEUS

Rather your eyes must with his **judgment** look.

HERMIA

I do **entreat** your grace to **pardon** me.
I know not by what power I am made bold,
Nor how it may **concern** my modesty
In such a **presence** here to **plead** my thoughts:
But I **beseech** your grace that I may know

Italian

according: secondo.
ancient: antico.
beg: mendicare, mendicano, mendica, mendicate, mendico, mendichiamo, mendichi, chiedere, elemosinare, supplicare.
beseech: supplicare, scongiurare, implorare.
concern: riguardare, concernere, cura, azienda, importanza, preoccupazione.
disfigure: sfigurare, sfiguriamo,

sfiguri, sfiguro, sfigurate, sfigurano, sfigura.
dispose: disporre, disponete, dispongo, dispongono, disponi, disponiamo.
entreat: supplicare.
figure: figura, calcolare, cifra, numero.
gentleman: signore, galantuomo, gentiluomo.
judgment: giudizio, sentenza.
mine: miniera, mina, minare, estrarre.
pardon: grazia, perdono, perdonare,

scusare, scusa.
plead: peroro, supplico, supplichiamo, supplichi, supplicate, supplica, peroriamo, perori, perorano, perora, imploro.
presence: presenza.
privilege: privilegio, privilegiare.
provided: provvisto, fornito.
wanting: volendo.
whom: chi, cui.
worthy: degno, meritevole.

The worst that may **befall** me in this case
If I **refuse** to wed Demetrius.

THESEUS
Either to die the death, or to abjure
For ever the society of men.
Therefore, fair Hermia, question your desires,
Know of your youth, examine well your blood,
Whether, if you **yield** not to your father's choice,
You can **endure** the **livery** of a nun;
For aye to be **shady cloister** mew'd,
To live a **barren** sister all your life,
Chanting **faint** hymns to the cold, **fruitless** moon.
Thrice-blessed they that master so their blood
To **undergo** such **maiden** pilgrimage:
But earthlier happy is the rose distill'd
Than that which, withering on the **virgin** thorn,
Grows, lives, and **dies**, in single **blessedness**.

HERMIA
So will I grow, so live, so die, my lord,
Ere I will yield my virgin **patent** up
Unto his **lordship**, whose unwished yoke
My soul consents not to give **sovereignty**.

THESEUS
Take time to **pause**; and by the next new moon,--
The sealing-day **betwixt** my love and me
For **everlasting bond** of fellowship,--
Upon that day either prepare to die
For **disobedience** to your father's will;
Or else to wed Demetrius, as he would;
Or on Diana's **altar** to protest
For aye **austerity** and single life.

Italian

altar: altare.
austerity: austerità.
barren: sterile.
befall: succedete, succedi, succediamo, succedo, succedono, succedere.
betwixt: tra.
blessedness: beatitudine.
bond: legame, obbligazione, collegare, vincolo.
cloister: chiostro.
dies: muore.
disobedience: disubbidienza.

endure: sopportare, sopporta, sopporto, sopportiamo, sopporti, sopportano, sopportate, tollerare, durare, duriamo, dura.
everlasting: eterno.
faint: debole, svenire, svengo, svengono, sveniamo, svenite, svieni, svenimento, vago.
fruitless: infruttuoso, inutile.
livery: livrea.
lordship: signoria, dominio.
maiden: nubile, fanciulla.

patent: brevetto, brevettato, palese, brevettare.
pause: pausa, sosta.
refuse: rifiutare, rifiutarsi, rifiuti.
shady: ombreggiato.
sovereignty: sovranità.
undergo: subire, subisci, subisco, subiscono, subite, subiamo.
virgin: vergine.
yield: cedere, cedete, cedi, cediamo, cedo, cedono, resa, rendimento, prodotto, fruttare.

A Midsummer Night's Dream

DEMETRIUS

    Relent, **sweet** Hermia;--and, Lysander, yield
    Thy crazed **title** to my certain right.

LYSANDER

    You have her father's love, Demetrius;
    Let me have Hermia's: do you **marry** him.

EGEUS

    Scornful Lysander! **true**, he hath my love;
    And what is **mine** my love shall **render** him;
    And she is mine; and all my right of her
    I do **estate unto** Demetrius.

LYSANDER

    I am, my **lord**, as well deriv'd as he,
    As well possess'd; my love is more than his;
    My fortunes every way as **fairly** rank'd,
    If not with **vantage**, as Demetrius's;
    And, which is more than all these boasts can be,
    I am belov'd of beauteous Hermia:
    Why should not I then **prosecute** my right?
    Demetrius, I'll **avouch** it to his head,
    Made love to Nedar's **daughter**, Helena,
    And **won** her **soul**; and she, sweet **lady**, dotes,
    Devoutly dotes, dotes in idolatry,
    Upon this **spotted** and **inconstant** man.

THESEUS

    I must **confess** that I have **heard** so much,
    And with Demetrius thought to have **spoke** thereof;
    But, being over-full of self-affairs,
    My mind did **lose** it.--But, Demetrius, come;
    And come, Egeus; you shall go with me;
    I have some **private schooling** for you both.--

Italian

avouch: garantire.
confess: confessare, confessa, confessano, confessate, confessi, confessiamo, confesso.
daughter: figlia, figliola, figliuola, la figlia.
estate: fattoria, patrimonio, tenuta.
fairly: abbastanza, equamente.
heard: udito, sentito.
inconstant: incostante.
lady: signora, dama.
lord: signore.

lose: perdere, perdiamo, perdete, perdi, perdo, perdono.
marry: sposare, sposati, sposatevi, si sposi, si sposate, si sposano, ci sposiamo, mi sposo, maritarsi, ammogliarsi, maritare.
mine: miniera, mina, minare, estrarre.
private: privato, senza impiego, riservato.
prosecute: perseguire, persegui, perseguiamo, perseguite, perseguo, perseguono, perseguitare.

render: rendere, rendono, rendete, rendi, rendiamo, rendo.
schooling: istruzione.
soul: anima.
spoke: raggio.
spotted: maculato.
sweet: dolce, soave, caramella.
title: titolo.
true: vero.
unto: a.
vantage: vantaggio.
won: vinto.

For you, fair Hermia, look you **arm** yourself
To **fit** your fancies to your father's will,
Or else the law of Athens **yields** you up,--
Which by no means we may extenuate,--
To death, or to a **vow** of single life.--
Come, my Hippolyta: what **cheer**, my love?
Demetrius, and Egeus, go along;
I must **employ** you in some business
Against our nuptial, and **confer** with you
Of something **nearly** that concerns yourselves.

EGEUS

With **duty** and **desire** we **follow** you.

[Exeunt THESEUS, HIPPOLYTA, EGEUS, DEMETRIUS, and **Train.**]

LYSANDER

How now, my love! why is your **cheek** so pale?
How **chance** the roses there do **fade** so **fast**?

HERMIA

Belike for want of rain, which I could well
Beteem them from the **tempest** of my eyes.

LYSANDER

Ah me! for aught that I could ever read,
Could ever hear by **tale** or history,
The course of true love never did run smooth:
But either it was different in blood,--

HERMIA

O **cross**! Too high to be enthrall'd to low!

LYSANDER

Or else misgraffed in **respect** of years;--

HERMIA

O **spite**! Too old to be engag'd to young!

Italian

arm: armare, braccio, arma, il braccio, armi.
chance: caso.
cheek: guancia, la guancia.
cheer: rallegrare.
confer: conferire, conferiamo, conferisci, conferiscono, conferite, conferisco.
cross: croce, attraversare, irato, incrociare, incrocio, varcare, valicare, traversare, accavallare.
desire: desiderio, desiderare, bramare.

duty: dovere, dazio, imposta, mansione.
employ: usare, impiegare, assumere, occupare.
fade: dissolvenza, svanire, svanisci, svanite, svanisco, svaniamo, svaniscono, sbiadire, avvizzire, appassire.
fast: veloce, digiuno, velocemente, presto, digiunare, rapido.
fit: adattare, aggiustare, apoplessia, in forma, adatto.

follow: seguire, seguiamo, seguite, seguo, seguono, segui.
low: basso.
nearly: quasi.
rain: pioggia, piovere, la pioggia.
respect: rispettare, rispetto, stima.
spite: dispetto.
tale: racconto, storia, novella, favola.
tempest: tempesta.
vow: voto.
yields: cede.

LYSANDER

Or else it stood upon the choice of friends:

HERMIA

O **hell**! to choose love by another's eye!

LYSANDER

Or, if there were a **sympathy** in choice,
War, death, or **sickness**, did lay **siege** to it,
Making it **momentary** as a sound,
Swift as a **shadow**, short as any dream;
Brief as the **lightning** in the collied night
That, in a **spleen**, **unfolds** both heaven and earth,
And ere a man hath power to say, Behold!
The **jaws** of **darkness** do **devour** it up:
So **quick bright** things come to confusion.

HERMIA

If then true lovers have ever cross'd,
It stands as an **edict** in destiny:
Then let us **teach** our **trial** patience,
Because it is a **customary** cross;
As due to love as thoughts, and dreams, and sighs,
Wishes and **tears**, poor fancy's **followers**.

LYSANDER

A good **persuasion**; therefore, hear me, Hermia.
I have a **widow aunt**, a dowager
Of great revenue, and she hath no child:
From Athens is her house **remote** seven leagues;
And she respects me as her only son.
There, **gentle** Hermia, may I marry thee;
And to that place the **sharp** Athenian law
Cannot **pursue** us. If thou lovest me then,
Steal forth thy father's house tomorrow night;

Italian

aunt: zia, la zia.
bright: brillante, luminoso, splendente, chiaro.
customary: consueto, usuale, abituale.
darkness: oscurità, tenebre.
devour: divorare, divorano, divora, divorate, divoriamo, divoro, divori.
edict: editto.
followers: seguito.
gentle: mite, gentile, dolce, delicato.
hell: inferno.
jaws: ganasce.

lightning: fulmine, baleno, lampo.
momentary: momentaneo.
persuasion: persuasione.
pursue: perseguire, persegui, perseguite, perseguo, perseguiamo, perseguono, perseguitare, inseguire.
quick: rapido, svelto, veloce.
remote: distante, lontano, remoto, isolato, a distanza, periferico.
shadow: ombra.
sharp: affilato, aguzzo, acuto, tagliente, appuntito, piccante, giusto,

giustamente, aspro, diesis, nitido.
sickness: malattia.
siege: assedio.
spleen: milza, malumore.
sympathy: compassione.
teach: insegnare, insegna, insegnano, insegniamo, insegni, insegnate, insegno, istruire.
tears: lacrime.
trial: prova, esperimento.
unfolds: spiega.
widow: vedova.

And in the **wood**, a league without the town,
Where I did meet thee once with Helena,
To do **observance** to a **morn** of May,
There will I stay for thee.

HERMIA
My good Lysander!
I **swear** to thee by Cupid's strongest bow,
By his best **arrow**, with the **golden** head,
By the **simplicity** of Venus' doves,
By that which knitteth souls and **prospers loves**,
And by that fire which burn'd the Carthage queen,
When the **false** Trojan under **sail** was seen,--
By all the vows that ever men have broke,
In number more than ever women spoke,--
In that same place thou hast **appointed** me,
Tomorrow **truly** will I meet with thee.

LYSANDER
Keep **promise**, love. Look, here comes Helena.

[**Enter** HELENA.]

HERMIA
God **speed** fair Helena! **Whither** away?

HELENA
Call you me fair? that fair again unsay.
Demetrius loves your fair. O happy fair!
Your eyes are lode-stars; and your **tongue's** sweet air
More tuneable than **lark** to shepherd's ear,
When **wheat** is green, when **hawthorn** buds appear.
Sickness is **catching**: O, were **favour** so,
Yours would I catch, fair Hermia, ere I go;
My ear should catch your voice, my eye your eye,
My tongue should catch your tongue's sweet melody.

Italian

appointed: nominato.
arrow: freccia, saetta.
catch: prendere, prendi, prendono, prendete, prendiamo, prendo, fermo, colpire, colpiscono, colpisco, colpiamo.
catching: contagioso, prendendo, infettivo, colpendo, prendere.
ear: orecchio, spiga, l'orecchio, pannocchia.
enter: entrare, entra, entrano, entrate, entri, entriamo, entro, invio.

false: falso, finto.
favour: favorire, favore.
golden: dorato, aureo, d'oro.
hawthorn: biancospino.
lark: allodola.
loves: amore.
morn: mattino.
observance: osservanza.
promise: promessa, promettere, promettono, promettete, prometti, promettiamo, prometto.
prospers: prospera.

sail: vela, veleggiare, la vela, salpare, navigare.
simplicity: semplicità.
speed: velocità, andatura, rapidità.
swear: giurare, giura, giuro, giuriamo, giuri, giurano, giurate, bestemmiare, imprecare.
tongue: lingua, linguetta, la lingua.
truly: davvero, infatti, veramente.
wheat: frumento, grano.
whither: dove.
wood: legno, bosco, selva, legna.

Were the world **mine**, Demetrius being bated,
The **rest** I'd give to be to you translated.
O, **teach** me how you look; and with what art
You **sway** the **motion** of Demetrius' **heart**!

HERMIA

I **frown** upon him, yet he **loves** me still.

HELENA

O that your frowns would teach my smiles such **skill**!

HERMIA

I give him curses, yet he **gives** me love.

HELENA

O that my **prayers** could such **affection move**!

HERMIA

The more I **hate**, the more he **follows** me.

HELENA

The more I love, the more he hateth me.

HERMIA

His **folly**, Helena, is no **fault** of mine.

HELENA

None, but your **beauty**: would that fault were mine!

HERMIA

Take **comfort**; he no more shall see my face;
Lysander and **myself** will **fly** this place.--
Before the time I did Lysander see,
Seem'd Athens as a **paradise** to me:
O, then, what graces in my love do dwell,
That he hath turn'd a **heaven unto hell**!

LYSANDER

Helen, to you our minds we will unfold:

Italian

affection: affetto, affezione, amore.
beauty: bellezza.
comfort: consolare, comodità, confortare, comfort, benessere.
fault: difetto, faglia, guasto, fallo.
fly: volare, voli, volate, voliamo, vola, volo, volano, mosca.
follows: segue.
folly: follia.
frown: cipiglio.
gives: dà, regala.
hate: odiare, odio, detestare.

heart: cuore, il cuore.
heaven: cielo, paradiso.
hell: inferno.
loves: amore.
mine: miniera, mina, minare, estrarre.
motion: movimento, mozione, moto.
move: muovere, muoversi, spostare, mossa, movimento, traslocare, trasportare, trasferire, commuovere.
myself: mi, me stesso, io stesso.
paradise: paradiso.
prayers: preghiere.

rest: riposo, riposarsi, riposare, resto, pausa.
skill: abilità, destrezza, maestria.
sway: oscillare, ondeggiare, barcollare, oscillazione.
teach: insegnare, insegna, insegnano, insegniamo, insegni, insegnate, insegno, istruire.
unto: a.

To-morrow night, when Phoebe doth behold
Her silver **visage** in the **watery** glass,
Decking with **liquid pearl** the bladed grass,--
A time that lovers' flights doth **still** conceal,--
Through Athens' gates have we devis'd to steal.

HERMIA

And in the wood where often you and I
Upon faint **primrose beds** were **wont** to lie,
Emptying our bosoms of their **counsel** sweet,
There my Lysander and myself shall meet:
And **thence** from Athens **turn** away our eyes,
To **seek** new **friends** and **stranger** companies.
Farewell, sweet **playfellow: pray** thou for us,
And good **luck grant** thee thy Demetrius!--
Keep word, Lysander: we must **starve** our sight
From lovers' **food**, till **morrow deep midnight**.

LYSANDER

I will, my Hermia.

[**Exit** HERMIA.]

LYSANDER

Helena, adieu:
As you on him, Demetrius **dote** on you!

[Exit LYSANDER.]

HELENA

How happy some o'er other some can be!
Through Athens I am thought as fair as she.
But what of that? Demetrius **thinks** not so;
He will not know what all but he do know.
And as he **errs**, doting on Hermia's eyes,
So I, **admiring** of his qualities.

Italian

admiring: ammirando, ammirativo.
beds: letti.
counsel: consiglio, avvocato, consigliare, raccomandare, avviso.
deep: profondo, fondo, intenso, cupo.
dote: essere rimbambito.
errs: erra.
exit: uscita, uscire, l'uscita.
food: cibo, alimento, generi alimentari, vivanda.
friends: amici.
grant: concessione, accordare,

sovvenzione.
liquid: liquido.
luck: fortuna.
midnight: mezzanotte.
morrow: domani.
pearl: perla.
playfellow: compagno di giochi.
pray: pregare, pregate, prego, preghi, prega, preghiamo, pregano.
primrose: primula.
seek: cercare, cercano, cerchiamo, cercate, cerchi, cerco, cerca.

starve: affamare.
stranger: sconosciuto, estraneo, forestiero.
thence: di là.
thinks: pensa.
till: finchè, coltivare, cassa, fino, arare.
turn: girare, giro, svoltare, gira, giriamo, giri, girate, girano, svolta, rovesciare, svoltiamo.
visage: viso, volto.
watery: acquoso.
wont: avvezzo, abitudine.

Things base and **vile**, **holding** no quantity,
Love can **transpose** to form and dignity.
Love **looks** not with the eyes, but with the mind;
And therefore is wing'd Cupid **painted** blind.
Nor hath love's mind of any **judgment** taste;
Wings and no eyes **figure** unheedy haste:
And therefore is love said to be a child,
Because in **choice** he is so **oft** beguil'd.
As **waggish boys** in **game** themselves forswear,
So the boy Love is perjur'd everywhere:
For ere Demetrius look'd on Hermia's eyne,
He **hail'd** down **oaths** that he was only mine;
And when this hail some **heat** from Hermia felt,
So he dissolv'd, and showers of oaths did melt.
I will go tell him of **fair** Hermia's flight;
Then to the **wood** will he to-morrow night
Pursue her; and for this intelligence
If I have **thanks**, it is a **dear** expense:
But **herein** mean I to **enrich** my pain,
To have his **sight thither** and back again.
[**Exit** HELENA.]

SCENE II. THE SAME. A ROOM IN A COTTAGE.

[Enter SNUG, BOTTOM, FLUTE, SNOUT, QUINCE, and STARVELING.]
QUINCE
    Is all our company here?

Italian

boy: ragazzo, servire.
choice: scelta.
dear: caro, costoso, egregio.
enrich: arricchire, arricchiscono, arricchite, arricchisco, arricchisci, arricchiamo.
exit: uscita, uscire, l'uscita.
fair: biondo, fiera, giusto, bazar, correttamente, bello, equo.
figure: figura, calcolare, cifra, numero.
game: gioco, giuoco, cacciagione, selvaggina, partita.

hail: grandine, grandinare.
heat: calore, riscaldare, ardore, caldo, scaldare.
herein: qui.
holding: tenere, tenuta, detenzione, podere, presa.
judgment: giudizio, sentenza.
looks: guarda.
oaths: giuramenti.
oft: spesso.
painted: dipinto, verniciato.
sight: vista, aspetto, avvistare, aria,

apparenza.
thanks: grazie, ringrazia.
thither: là.
transpose: trasporre.
vile: abietto.
waggish: scherzoso.
wood: legno, bosco, selva, legna.

BOTTOM

You were best to **call** them **generally**, man by man,
according to the scrip.

QUINCE

Here is the **scroll** of every man's name, which is thought
fit, through all Athens, to play in our **interlude** before the
duke and **duchess** on his wedding-day at night.

BOTTOM

First, good Peter Quince, say what the play **treats** on;
then read the **names** of the **actors**; and so **grow** to a point.

QUINCE

Marry, our play is--The most **lamentable comedy** and most
cruel death of Pyramus and Thisby.

BOTTOM

A very good **piece** of work, I **assure** you, and a merry.--
Now, good Peter Quince, call forth your actors by the scroll.--
Masters, **spread yourselves**.

QUINCE

Answer, as I call you.--Nick Bottom, the **weaver**.

BOTTOM

Ready. Name what part I am for, and **proceed**.

QUINCE

You, Nick Bottom, are set down for Pyramus.

BOTTOM

What is Pyramus? a **lover**, or a **tyrant**?

QUINCE

A lover, that kills himself most **gallantly** for love.

BOTTOM

That will **ask** some tears in the true **performing** of it. If I do it, let the

Italian

actors: attori.
ask: chiedere, chiedi, chiediamo, chiedo, chiedete, chiedono, domandare, domando, domandate, domandi, domandiamo.
assure: assicurare, assicura, assicuriamo, assicurate, assicuri, assicurano, assicuro, garantire.
call: chiamare, chiami, chiamiamo, chiamo, chiamano, chiama, chiamate, chiamata, appello.
comedy: commedia.

duchess: duchessa.
gallantly: galantemente.
generally: generalmente.
grow: crescere, crescete, crescono, cresco, cresci, cresciamo, coltivare, coltiviamo, coltivo, coltivi, coltivate.
interlude: intermezzo, interludio, intervallo.
lamentable: lamentevole, deplorevole.
lover: amante.
names: nomi.
performing: eseguendo.

piece: pezzo, parte, porzione.
proceed: procedere, procedete, procedono, procedo, procediamo, procedi.
scroll: rotolo di pergamena, scorrere.
spread: diffondere, spargere, diffusione, spalmare, propagare, scarto.
treats: leccornie.
tyrant: tiranno.
weaver: tessitore.
yourselves: voi stessi.

audience look to their eyes; I will move storms; I will condole in some **measure**. To the rest:--yet my **chief humour** is for a tyrant: I could play Ercles **rarely**, or a part to **tear** a **cat** in, to make all split.

    The **raging** rocks
    And **shivering** shocks
    Shall **break** the locks
    Of **prison** gates:
    And Phibbus' car
    Shall **shine** from far,
    And make and mar
    The **foolish** Fates.

This was lofty.--Now name the rest of the players.--This is Ercles' **vein**, a tyrant's vein;--a lover is more condoling.

QUINCE

Francis Flute, the bellows-mender.

FLUTE

Here, Peter Quince.

QUINCE

Flute, you must take Thisby on you.

FLUTE

What is Thisby? a **wandering knight**?

QUINCE

It is the lady that Pyramus must love.

FLUTE

Nay, **faith**, let not me play a woman; I have a **beard coming**.

QUINCE

That's all one; you shall play it in a **mask**, and you may **speak** as small as you will.

BOTTOM

An I may **hide** my face, let me play Thisby too: I'll speak in a **monstrous** little

---

Italian

audience: udienza, uditorio, pubblico.
beard: barba.
break: rompere, rottura, spezzare, rompersi, frattura, pausa, schiantare, infrangere, sosta, spaccare.
cat: gatto, il gatto.
chief: capo, principale.
coming: venendo.
faith: fede, fiducia.
foolish: sciocco, stupido, stolto, ignorante, fesso.
hide: nascondere, nascondo,

nascondiamo, nascondono, nascondete, nascondi, pelle, nascondersi, pellame, celare, occultare.
humour: umore, umorismo.
knight: cavaliere, cavallo.
mask: maschera, mascherare, mascherina.
measure: misura, misurare, provvedimento.
monstrous: mostruoso.
prison: prigione, carcere.

raging: furente, infuriato, furioso.
rarely: raramente.
shine: risplendere, brillare, lustro, splendere.
shivering: rabbrividire.
speak: parlare, parla, parlo, parliamo, parli, parlate, parlano, favellare.
tear: strappo, lagrima, strappare, lacerare, lacrima.
vein: vena.
wandering: vagando, peregrinazione.

voice;--'Thisne, Thisne!'-- 'Ah, Pyramus, my **lover dear**; **thy** Thisby dear! and **lady** dear!'

QUINCE

No, no, you must **play** Pyramus; and, Flute, you Thisby.

BOTTOM

Well, **proceed**.

QUINCE

Robin Starveling, the **tailor**.

STARVELING

Here, Peter Quince.

QUINCE

Robin Starveling, you must play Thisby's mother.--Tom Snout, the tinker.

SNOUT

Here, Peter Quince.

QUINCE

You, Pyramus' father; myself, Thisby's father;--Snug, the **joiner**, you, the **lion's** part:--and, I **hope**, here is a play **fitted**.

SNUG

Have you the lion's part **written**? **pray** you, if it be, give it me, for I am **slow** of study.

QUINCE

You may do it **extempore**, for it is nothing but **roaring**.

BOTTOM

Let me play the lion too: I will roar that I will do any man's **heart** good to hear me; I will roar that I will make the **duke** say 'Let him roar again, let him roar again.'

QUINCE

An you should do it too **terribly**, you would **fright** the **duchess** and the **ladies**, that they would **shriek**; and that were enough to **hang** us all.

Italian

dear: caro, costoso, egregio.
duchess: duchessa.
duke: duca.
extempore: estemporaneo.
fitted: aderente, adatto, attrezzato.
fright: paura, spavento, timore, angoscia.
hang: pendere, appendere, sospendere, impiccare.
hear: udire, odono, odi, odo, udite, udiamo, sentire, sentono, sento, sentite, senti.

hope: speranza, sperare, spera, sperano, sperate, speri, speriamo, spero.
joiner: falegname.
ladies: signore.
lady: signora, dama.
lion: leone.
lover: amante.
play: giocare, giocano, giocate, giochiamo, gioca, giochi, gioco, suonare, suona, suoni, suoniamo.
pray: pregare, pregate, prego, preghi,

prega, preghiamo, pregano.
proceed: procedere, procedete, procedono, procedo, procediamo, procedi.
roar: ruggire, muggire, ruggito, scrosciare.
shriek: strillo, strillare.
slow: lento.
tailor: sarto.
terribly: terribilmente.
thy: tuo.
written: scritto.

ALL

That would hang us every mother's son.

BOTTOM

I grant you, friends, if you should fright the ladies out of their wits, they would have no more **discretion** but to hang us: but I will **aggravate** my voice so, that I will roar you as **gently** as any **sucking dove**; I will roar you an 'twere any **nightingale**.

QUINCE

You can play no part but Pyramus; for Pyramus is a sweet-faced man; a **proper** man, as one shall see in a summer's day; a most **lovely** gentleman-like man; therefore you must needs play Pyramus.

BOTTOM

Well, I will **undertake** it. What beard were I best to play it in?

QUINCE

Why, what you will.

BOTTOM

I will **discharge** it in either your straw-colour beard, your orange-tawny beard, your purple-in-grain beard, or your French-crown-colour beard, your **perfect yellow**.

QUINCE

Some of your French crowns have no hair at all, and then you will play bare-faced.-- But, masters, here are your **parts**: and I am to entreat you, **request** you, and desire you, to **con** them by to-morrow night; and meet me in the **palace** wood, a **mile** without the town, by moonlight; there will we **rehearse**: for if we meet in the city, we shall be dogg'd with company, and our **devices** known. In the **meantime** I will draw a bill of properties, such as our play **wants**. I pray you, **fail** me not.

BOTTOM

We will meet; and there we may rehearse most obscenely and **courageously**. Take **pains**; be perfect; **adieu**.

Italian

adieu: addio.
aggravate: aggravare, aggravo, aggrava, aggravano, aggravate, aggravi, aggraviamo, peggiorare.
con: contro.
courageously: coraggiosamente.
devices: dispositivi.
discharge: scarico, scarica, portata, scaricare.
discretion: discrezione.
dove: colomba, piccione.
fail: fallire, morire, mancare.

gently: delicatamente.
lovely: bello, piacevole, amabile, grazioso, gradevole, affascinante, caro, carino.
meantime: frattanto, nel frattempo, intanto.
mile: miglio.
nightingale: usignolo.
pains: dolori.
palace: palazzo, il palazzo.
parts: ricambi, parte.
perfect: perfetto, perfezionare.

proper: decente, proprio.
rehearse: proviamo, provo, provi, provate, provano, provare, prova.
request: richiesta, richiedere, chiedere, domanda.
sucking: aspirante, succhiare.
undertake: intraprendere, intraprendete, intraprendono, intraprendo, intraprendi, intraprendiamo.
wants: vuole.
yellow: giallo.

QUINCE
At the duke's **oak** we meet.

BOTTOM
Enough; **hold**, or **cut** bow-strings.

[Exeunt.]

Italian

cut: taglio, tagliare, tagliato, taglia, incisione.
hold: tenere, stiva, stretta, mantenere, ritenere.
oak: quercia.

ACT II

SCENE I. A WOOD NEAR ATHENS.

[Enter a FAIRY at One door, and PUCK at another.]

PUCK

How now, **spirit**! **whither wander** you?

FAIRY

Over **hill**, over dale,
Thorough **bush**, **thorough** brier,
Over **park**, over pale,
Thorough **flood**, thorough fire,
I do wander everywhere,
Swifter than the moon's sphere;
And I **serve** the **fairy** queen,
To **dew** her orbs upon the green.
The cowslips **tall** her pensioners be:
In their **gold** coats spots you see;
Those be rubies, fairy favours,
In those freckles **live** their savours;
I must go **seek** some dew-drops here,

Italian

bush: arbusto, cespuglio, boccola, bussola.
dew: rugiada.
fairy: fata.
flood: inondazione, alluvione, allagare, alta marea, inondare, diluvio, sommergere, allagamento, piena.
gold: oro, d'oro.
hill: collina, colle, altura.
live: vivere, vivete, vivono, viviamo, vivi, vivo, abitare, abiti, abita,

abitano, abitate.
park: parco, parcheggiare.
seek: cercare, cercano, cerchiamo, cercate, cerchi, cerco, cerca.
serve: servire, serviamo, servi, servono, servite, servo.
spirit: spirito, anima.
tall: alto, grande, elevato.
thorough: completo, accurato.
wander: vagare, vago, errare, vaghiamo, vaga, vagano, vaghi, vagate, vagabondare.

whither: dove.

And hang a pearl in every cowslip's ear.
Farewell, thou lob of spirits; I'll be gone:
Our **queen** and all her elves come here anon.

PUCK

The king doth keep his revels here to-night;
Take **heed** the Queen come not within his sight.
For Oberon is **passing** fell and wrath,
Because that she, as her **attendant**, hath
A lovely boy, stol'n from an Indian king;
She never had so sweet a changeling:
And **jealous** Oberon would have the child
Knight of his **train**, to **trace** the forests wild:
But she **perforce withholds** the **loved** boy,
Crowns him with **flowers**, and makes him all her joy:
And now they never meet in **grove** or green,
By **fountain** clear, or spangled **starlight** sheen,
But they do **square**; that all their elves for fear
Creep into **acorn cups**, and hide them there.

FAIRY

Either I **mistake** your **shape** and making quite,
Or else you are that **shrewd** and **knavish** sprite
Call'd Robin Goodfellow: are not you he
That frights the maidens of the villagery;
Skim **milk**, and sometimes labour in the quern,
And bootless make the **breathless housewife** churn;
And sometime make the **drink** to **bear** no barm;
Mislead night-wanderers, **laughing** at their harm?
Those that Hobgoblin call you, and sweet Puck,
You do their work, and they shall have good luck:
Are not you he?

Italian

acorn: ghianda.
attendant: custode, compagno, inserviente.
bear: orso, produrre, ribassista, partorire, l'orso, portare.
breathless: ansante, senza fiato.
cups: tazza.
drink: bere, bevanda, bibita.
flowers: fiore.
fountain: fontana, sorgente, fonte.
grove: boschetto.
heed: cura, attenzione.

housewife: casalinga, massaia.
jealous: geloso.
knavish: furfantesco, da briccone, disonesto.
laughing: ridere, risata.
loved: benvoluto.
milk: latte, mungere, il latte.
mistake: errore, sbaglio, sbagliare, confondere, fallo.
passing: passeggero, passare, passaggio.
perforce: necessariamente.

queen: regina.
shape: forma, formare, figura, foggia, modellare, sagoma.
shrewd: scaltro, sagace, perspicace, accorto.
square: quadrato, piazza, quadro, squadra.
starlight: luce stellare, luce delle stelle.
trace: traccia, tracciare, delimitare.
train: treno, addestrare, il treno, ammaestrare, educare.
withholds: trattiene.

PUCK
                    Thou speak'st aright;
        I am that **merry wanderer** of the night.
        I **jest** to Oberon, and make him smile,
        When I a **fat** and bean-fed **horse** beguile,
        Neighing in **likeness** of a **filly** foal;
        And **sometime lurk** I in a gossip's bowl,
        In very likeness of a **roasted** crab;
        And, when she drinks, against her lips I bob,
        And on her **withered dewlap pour** the ale.
        The wisest aunt, **telling** the saddest tale,
        Sometime for three-foot **stool** mistaketh me;
        Then **slip** I from her **bum**, down **topples** she,
        And 'tailor' cries, and **falls** into a cough;
        And then the whole quire hold their hips and loffe,
        And **waxen** in their **mirth**, and neeze, and swear
        A merrier **hour** was never **wasted** there.--
        But room, **fairy**, here **comes** Oberon.

FAIRY
        And here my mistress.--Would that he were gone!
        [Enter OBERON at one door, with his Train, and TITANIA, at another, with
        hers.]

OBERON
        Ill met by **moonlight**, **proud** Titania.

TITANIA
        What, jealous Oberon! Fairies, **skip** hence;
        I have forsworn his **bed** and company.

OBERON
        Tarry, **rash wanton**: am not I **thy** lord?

TITANIA
        Then I must be thy lady; but I know

Italian

bed: letto, il letto.	**lurk**: nascondersi.	slittare, frana, ingobbio.
bum: scroccare.	**merry**: allegro, festoso, gaio.	**stool**: sgabello, feci.
comes: viene.	**met**: incontrato.	**telling**: dicendo, raccontando,
dewlap: giogaia.	**mirth**: gaiezza, allegria, ilarità, gioia.	narrando.
fairy: fata.	**moonlight**: chiaro di luna.	**thy**: tuo.
falls: cade.	**pour**: versare.	**topples**: crolla, rovescia.
fat: grasso, grosso, pingue, spesso.	**proud**: orgoglioso, fiero.	**wanderer**: vagabondo.
filly: puledra.	**rash**: eruzione, avventato, eruzione	**wanton**: sfrenato, scatenato,
horse: cavallo, il cavallo.	cutanea.	licenzioso.
hour: ora, l'ora.	**roasted**: arrostito.	**wasted**: sprecato.
jest: scherzare, scherzo.	**skip**: salto, saltellare.	**waxen**: cereo.
likeness: somiglianza, rassomiglianza.	**slip**: scivolare, slittamento, sottoveste,	**withered**: appassito.

When **thou** hast stol'n away from fairy-land,
And in the shape of Corin **sat** all day,
Playing on **pipes** of **corn**, and versing love
To **amorous** Phillida. Why **art** thou here,
Come from the **farthest steep** of India,
But that, forsooth, the **bouncing** Amazon,
Your buskin'd **mistress** and your **warrior** love,
To Theseus must be **wedded**; and you come
To give their bed **joy** and prosperity.

OBERON

How canst thou thus, for **shame**, Titania,
Glance at my **credit** with Hippolyta,
Knowing I know **thy** love to Theseus?
Didst not thou **lead** him through the glimmering night
From Perigenia, whom he ravish'd?
And make him with fair Aegle break his faith,
With Ariadne and Antiopa?

TITANIA

These are the forgeries of jealousy:
And never, since the **middle** summer's spring,
Met we on hill, in **dale**, **forest**, or mead,
By **paved fountain**, or by rushy brook,
Or on the beached margent of the sea,
To **dance** our ringlets to the **whistling** wind,
But with thy brawls thou hast disturb'd our sport.
Therefore the winds, **piping** to us in vain,
As in **revenge**, have suck'd up from the sea
Contagious fogs; which, **falling** in the land,
Hath every pelting **river** made so proud
That they have overborne their continents:
The **ox** hath therefore stretch'd his **yoke** in vain,

Italian

amorous: amoroso.
art: arte, l'arte.
bouncing: robusto, rimbalzare, grosso, rimbalzo.
corn: granturco, callo, mais, grano, granoturco, cereale.
credit: credito, accreditare, avere.
dale: valle.
dance: ballare, ballo, danza.
falling: cadendo.
farthest: il più lontano.
forest: bosco, foresta, selva.

fountain: fontana, sorgente, fonte.
joy: gioia.
lead: piombo, condurre, conduciamo, conducono, conduco, conducete, conduci, guidare, guidiamo, guidano, guidate.
middle: mezzo, medio, metà, di mezzo.
mistress: padrona.
ox: bue.
paved: pavimentato.
pipes: tubi.

piping: tubatura.
revenge: vendetta.
river: fiume.
sat: seduto, covato.
shame: vergogna, pudore.
steep: ripido, erto, scosceso.
thou: tu.
thy: tuo.
warrior: guerriero.
wedded: sposato.
whistling: fischiare
yoke: giogo, aggiogare.

The ploughman lost his **sweat**; and the green corn
Hath **rotted** ere his youth attain'd a beard:
The **fold** stands **empty** in the **drowned** field,
And crows are fatted with the murrion flock;
The nine men's morris is fill'd up with mud;
And the quaint mazes in the wanton green,
For lack of **tread**, are undistinguishable:
The human mortals want their winter here;
No night is now with **hymn** or carol blest:--
Therefore the moon, the **governess** of floods,
Pale in her **anger**, **washes** all the air,
That **rheumatic** diseases do abound:
And thorough this distemperature we see
The seasons **alter**: hoary-headed frosts
Fall in the fresh **lap** of the **crimson** rose;
And on old Hyem's **thin** and **icy** crown
An **odorous chaplet** of sweet summer buds
Is, as in **mockery**, set: the **spring**, the summer,
The childing **autumn**, **angry** winter, change
Their **wonted** liveries; and the maz'd world,
By their increase, now knows not which is which:
And this same **progeny** of evils comes
From our **debate**, from our dissension:
We are their parents and original.

OBERON

Do you **amend** it, then: it lies in you:
Why should Titania cross her Oberon?
I do but beg a little changeling boy
To be my **henchman**.

TITANIA

                    Set your heart at rest;

Italian

alter: cambiarsi, alterare, altera, alteriamo, alterano, alteri, alterate, altero, modificare, mutare, cambiare.
amend: emendare, emendo, emendiamo, emendi, emendate, emendano, emenda.
anger: collera, rabbia, ira.
angry: arrabbiato, irato, stizzito.
autumn: autunno, l'autunno.
chaplet: sopporto per anima, ghirlanda.
crimson: cremisi.

debate: dibattito, dibattere, discussione.
drowned: annegato.
empty: vuoto, vuotare, vacuo.
fold: piegare, piega, plica, ovile, grinza, stabbio.
governess: istitutrice, governante.
henchman: accolito.
hymn: inno.
icy: ghiacciato, gelato.
lap: lappare, grembo.
mockery: derisione.

odorous: odoroso.
progeny: progenie.
quaint: bizzarro, antiquato.
rheumatic: reumatico.
rotted: marcito.
spring: molla, sorgente, primavera, fonte, saltare, la primavera.
sweat: sudare, sudore, traspirare.
thin: magro, sottile.
tread: pedata, passo, battistrada.
washes: lava.
wonted: usuale, consueto, solito.

The **fairy**-land buys not the child of me.
His mother was a vot'ress of my order:
And, in the spiced Indian air, by night,
Full often hath she gossip'd by my side;
And sat with me on Neptune's yellow sands,
Marking the **embarked** traders on the flood;
When we have laugh'd to see the sails conceive,
And grow big-bellied with the **wanton** wind;
Which she, with **pretty** and with **swimming** gait
Following,--her **womb** then **rich** with my young squire,--
Would **imitate**; and sail upon the land,
To **fetch** me trifles, and **return** again,
As from a **voyage**, rich with merchandise.
But she, being **mortal**, of that boy did die;
And for her **sake** do I **rear** up her boy:
And for her sake I will not part with him.

OBERON
How long within this wood **intend** you **stay**?

TITANIA
Perchance till after Theseus' wedding-day.
If you will **patiently** dance in our round,
And see our **moonlight** revels, go with us;
If not, **shun** me, and I will **spare** your haunts.

OBERON
Give me that boy and I will go with thee.

TITANIA
Not for thy fairy **kingdom**. Fairies, away:
We shall **chide downright** if I **longer** stay.

[Exit TITANIA with her Train.]

Italian

air: aria.
chide: sgrida, sgrido, sgridiamo, sgridi, sgridano, sgridate, sgridare.
downright: completamente, schietto.
embarked: imbarcato.
fetch: portare, portiamo, porto, porti, portate, portano, porta, ottenere, andare a prendere.
imitate: imitare, imitano, imito, imitiamo, imitate, imita, imiti, contraffare.
intend: intendere, intendono, intendo,

intendete, intendiamo, intendi.
kingdom: regno, reame.
longer: oltre, più lungo.
moonlight: chiaro di luna.
mortal: mortale.
patiently: pazientemente.
pretty: grazioso, bellino, carino, bello.
rear: posteriore, retroguardia, retro.
return: ritorno, ritornare, restituire, rientro, contraccambiare, resa, rendere, rivenire, restituzione.
rich: ricco.

sake: causa.
shun: evitare, eviti, evitiamo, evitano, evita, evitate, evito.
spare: risparmiare, scorta.
stay: stare, sta', stanno, sto, state, stiamo, stai, restare, rimanere, soggiorno, resta.
swimming: nuotando, nuoto.
voyage: viaggio.
wanton: sfrenato, scatenato, licenzioso.
womb: utero, grembo.

OBERON

Well, go thy way: thou shalt not from this grove
Till I **torment** thee for this injury.--
My gentle Puck, come **hither**: thou **remember'st**
Since once I sat upon a promontory,
And heard a **mermaid**, on a dolphin's back,
Uttering such **dulcet** and **harmonious** breath,
That the **rude sea** grew **civil** at her song,
And certain **stars shot madly** from their spheres
To hear the sea-maid's music.

PUCK

I remember.

OBERON

That very time I saw,--but thou couldst not,--
Flying between the **cold** moon and the earth,
Cupid, all arm'd: a certain **aim** he took
At a fair vestal, throned by the west;
And loos'd his love-shaft smartly from his bow,
As it should **pierce** a **hundred thousand** hearts;
But I might see young Cupid's **fiery** shaft
Quench'd in the **chaste** beams of the **watery** moon;
And the **imperial** votaress **passed** on,
In maiden **meditation**, fancy-free.
Yet mark'd I where the **bolt** of Cupid **fell**:
It fell upon a little **western flower**,--
Before milk-white, now **purple** with love's wound,--
And maidens call it love-in-idleness.
Fetch me that flower, the **herb** I showed thee once:
The **juice** of it on **sleeping** eyelids laid
Will make or man or woman madly dote
Upon the next live **creature** that it sees.

Italian

aim: scopo, proposito.
bolt: bullone, chiavistello, catenaccio.
chaste: casto.
civil: civile.
cold: freddo, raffreddore.
creature: creatura.
dulcet: melodioso.
fell: abbattere.
fiery: infuocato.
flower: fiore, fiorire.
harmonious: armonioso, armonico.
herb: erba, erbe.

hither: qui, quà.
hundred: cento, centinaio.
imperial: imperiale.
juice: succo, sugo.
madly: pazzamente, follemente.
meditation: meditazione.
mermaid: sirena.
passed: passato.
pierce: perforare, perfora, perforo,
  perforiamo, perfori, perforate,
  perforano, trapassare.
purple: viola, porpora, rosso porpora.

remember: ricordare, ricordiamo,
  ricorda, ricordano, ricordate, ricordi,
  ricordo.
rude: scortese, rozzo, maleducato.
sea: mare.
shot: sparato, sparo, tiro, colpo, scatto.
sleeping: dormendo, addormentato.
stars: spighe.
thousand: mille.
torment: tormento.
watery: acquoso.
western: occidentale.

Fetch me this herb: and be thou here again
Ere the **leviathan** can **swim** a league.

PUCK

I'll put a **girdle** round about the earth
In **forty** minutes.

[Exit PUCK.]

OBERON

                Having once this juice,
I'll **watch** Titania when she is asleep,
And **drop** the **liquor** of it in her eyes:
The next thing then she **waking** looks upon,--
Be it on lion, bear, or **wolf**, or bull,
On **meddling monkey**, or on **busy** ape,--
She shall pursue it with the soul of love.
And ere I take this **charm** from off her sight,--
As I can take it with another herb,
I'll make her render up her **page** to me.
But who comes here? I am invisible;
And I will **overhear** their **conference**.

[Enter DEMETRIUS, HELENA following him.]

DEMETRIUS

I love thee not, therefore pursue me not.
Where is Lysander and fair Hermia?
The one I'll **slay**, the other slayeth me.
Thou told'st me they were stol'n into this wood,
And here am I, and wode within this wood,
Because I **cannot meet** with Hermia.
Hence, get thee **gone**, and follow me no more.

HELENA

You **draw** me, you hard-hearted adamant;

Italian

busy: occupato, affaccendato, indaffarato.
cannot: non potere.
charm: fascino, incanto.
conference: conferenza, congresso.
draw: disegnare, disegna, disegniamo, disegni, disegnate, disegnano, disegno, tirare, attrarre, sorteggio, eguaglianza.
drop: goccia, diminuire, abbassamento, abbassare, caduta.
forty: quaranta.

girdle: cintura.
gone: andato.
leviathan: leviatano.
liquor: liquore.
meddling: ingerenza.
meet: incontrare, incontra, incontriamo, incontri, incontrano, incontrate, incontro, confluire.
monkey: scimmia, la scimmia.
overhear: origlia, origliate, origlio, origli, origliano, origliamo, origliare, udire per caso.

page: pagina, valletto.
slay: uccidere, uccidete, uccidono, uccido, uccidiamo, uccidi, ammazzare, ammazza, ammazzo, ammazziamo, ammazzi.
swim: nuotare, nuoto, nuotiamo, nuoti, nuotate, nuota, nuotano, nuotata.
waking: svegliare.
watch: orologio, guardare, sorvegliare, guardia, sentinella, osservare.
wolf: lupo.

But yet you draw not **iron**, for my heart
Is true as **steel**. Leave you your power to draw,
And I shall have no power to follow you.

DEMETRIUS

Do I **entice** you? Do I speak you fair?
Or, rather, do I not in plainest truth
Tell you I do not, **nor** I **cannot** love you?

HELENA

And even for that do I love you the more.
I am your spaniel; and, Demetrius,
The more you **beat** me, I **will fawn** on you:
Use me but as your spaniel, **spurn** me, **strike** me,
Neglect me, lose me; only give me leave,
Unworthy as I am, to follow you.
What worser place can I **beg** in your love,
And yet a place of high respect with me,--
Than to be used as you use your **dog**?

DEMETRIUS

Tempt not too much the **hatred** of my spirit;
For I am **sick** when I do look on **thee**.

HELENA

And I am sick when I look not on you.

DEMETRIUS

You do **impeach** your **modesty** too much,
To leave the city, and **commit** yourself
Into the **hands** of one that loves you not;
To **trust** the **opportunity** of night,
And the ill counsel of a **desert** place,
With the rich worth of your **virginity**.

Italian

beat: battere, picchiare, sbattere, battimento, battito.
beg: mendicare, mendicando, mendica, mendicate, mendico, mendichiamo, mendichi, chiedere, elemosinare, supplicare.
cannot: non potere.
commit: commettere.
desert: deserto, abbandonare.
dog: cane, il cane.
entice: attirare.
fawn: cerbiatto.

hands: mani.
hatred: odio.
ill: malato, ammalato.
impeach: accusi, incrimino, incriminiamo, incrimini, incriminate, incriminano, incrimina, accusiamo, accusate, accusano, accusa.
iron: ferro, ferro da stiro, stirare.
modesty: modestia, verecondia.
nor: ne.
opportunity: opportunità, occasione.
sick: malato, ammalato.

spurn: rifiutare, ripulsa, rifiuto.
steel: acciaio, osso di balena, acciaiare, d'acciaio.
strike: picchiare, colpire, battere, sciopero, scioperare, fare sciopero.
thee: te.
trust: fiducia, trust, confidenza, affidamento.
virginity: verginità.
worth: valore.

HELENA

Your **virtue** is my **privilege** for that.
It is not night when I do see your face,
Therefore I think I am not in the night;
Nor doth this wood **lack** worlds of company;
For you, in my respect, are all the world:
Then how can it be said I am alone
When all the world is here to look on me?

DEMETRIUS

I'll run from **thee**, and **hide** me in the brakes,
And leave thee to the **mercy** of **wild** beasts.

HELENA

The wildest hath not such a heart as you.
Run when you will, the **story** shall be chang'd;
Apollo **flies**, and Daphne holds the chase;
The **dove pursues** the griffin; the **mild** hind
Makes speed to catch the tiger,--bootless speed,
When **cowardice** pursues and **valour** flies.

DEMETRIUS

I will not stay **thy** questions; let me go:
Or, if **thou** follow me, do not believe
But I shall do thee **mischief** in the wood.

HELENA

Ay, in the **temple**, in the **town**, the field,
You do me mischief. Fie, Demetrius!
Your wrongs do set a **scandal** on my sex:
We **cannot fight** for love as men may do:
We should be woo'd, and were not made to woo.
I'll follow thee, and make a **heaven** of hell,
To **die** upon the hand I love so well.

[Exeunt DEMETRIUS and HELENA.]

Italian

cannot: non potere.
cowardice: codardia, vigliaccheria.
die: morire, muoio, muori, muoiono, morite, moriamo, dado, cubo, matrice, stampo.
dove: colomba, piccione.
fight: combattere, duellare, lotta, lottare, battaglia, picchiarsi, combattimento.
flies: vola.
heaven: cielo, paradiso.
hide: nascondere, nascondo, nascondiamo, nascondono, nascondete, nascondi, pelle, nascondersi, pellame, celare, occultare.
lack: mancanza, mancare, manchiamo, manchi, mancate, manca, mancano, manco, difetto, carenza.
mercy: misericordia.
mild: mite, dolce.
mischief: birichinata.
privilege: privilegio, privilegiare.
pursues: persegue.
scandal: scandalo, maldicenza.
story: storia, piano, racconto.
temple: tempia, tempio.
thee: te.
thou: tu.
thy: tuo.
town: città.
valour: valore.
virtue: virtù.
wild: selvaggio, feroce, selvatico.

OBERON

Fare **thee** well, **nymph**: ere he do **leave** this grove,
Thou shalt **fly** him, and he shall seek **thy** love.--
[Re-enter PUCK.]
Hast **thou** the **flower** there? **Welcome**, wanderer.

PUCK

Ay, there it is.

OBERON

I **pray** thee give it me.
I know a **bank** whereon the wild **thyme** blows,
Where ox-lips and the **nodding violet** grows;
Quite over-canopied with **luscious** woodbine,
With **sweet** musk-roses, and with eglantine:
There **sleeps** Titania sometime of the night,
Lulled in these flowers with dances and delight;
And there the **snake** throws her enamell'd skin,
Weed **wide** enough to **wrap** a **fairy** in:
And with the **juice** of this I'll **streak** her eyes,
And make her full of **hateful** fantasies.
Take thou some of it, and seek through this grove:
A sweet Athenian lady is in love
With a **disdainful** youth: **anoint** his eyes;
But do it when the next thing he espies
May be the lady: thou shalt know the man
By the Athenian **garments** he hath on.
Effect it with some care, that he may prove
More **fond** on her than she upon her love:
And look thou meet me ere the first **cock crow**.

PUCK

Fear not, my lord; your **servant** shall do so.

[Exeunt.]

Italian

anoint: ungere.
bank: banca, banco, la banca, sponda, riva.
cock: gallo, cazzo, rubinetto.
crow: cornacchia, corvo.
disdainful: sdegnoso, sprezzante.
fairy: fata.
flower: fiore, fiorire.
fly: volare, voli, volate, voliamo, vola, volo, volano, mosca.
fond: tenero, affettuoso, affezionato.
garments: indumenti.

hateful: odioso.
juice: succo, sugo.
leave: lasciare, abbandonare, partire, lasciano, partono, partite, partiamo, parti, lasciate, lasciamo, lascia.
luscious: delizioso, succulento.
nodding: cenno del capo.
nymph: ninfa.
pray: pregare, pregate, prego, preghi, prega, preghiamo, pregano.
servant: servire, servo, servitore.
sleeps: dorme.

snake: serpente.
streak: stria, striscia.
sweet: dolce, soave, caramella.
thee: te.
thou: tu.
thy: tuo.
thyme: timo.
violet: viola, violetta.
welcome: benvenuto, bene arrivate, accoglienza, gradito, accogliere.
wide: largo, vasto, ampio.
wrap: avvolgere.

SCENE II. ANOTHER PART OF THE WOOD.

[Enter TITANIA, with her Train.]

TITANIA

Come, now a roundel and a **fairy** song;
Then, for the third part of a **minute**, hence;
Some to **kill** cankers in the musk-rose buds;
Some war with rere-mice for their leathern wings,
To make my small elves coats; and some keep back
The **clamorous owl**, that **nightly** hoots and wonders
At our **quaint** spirits. **Sing** me now asleep;
Then to your **offices**, and let me **rest**.

SONG.

FIRST FAIRY

You **spotted** snakes, with **double** tongue,
Thorny hedgehogs, be not seen;
Newts and blind-worms do no wrong;
Come not **near** our fairy **queen**:

CHORUS.

Philomel, with melody,
Sing in our **sweet lullaby**:
Lulla, lulla, lullaby; lulla, lulla, lullaby:
Never **harm, nor spell**, nor charm,
Come our **lovely lady** nigh;
So good-night, with lullaby.

SECOND FAIRY

Weaving spiders, come not here;
Hence, you long-legg'd spinners, hence;

Italian

clamorous: clamoroso.
double: doppio, sosia, raddoppiare, duplice.
fairy: fata.
harm: danno, nuocere, danneggiare.
kill: uccidere, ammazzare.
lady: signora, dama.
lovely: bello, piacevole, amabile, grazioso, gradevole, affascinante, caro, carino.
lullaby: ninnananna.
minute: minuto, il minuto, minuscolo,

momento.
near: vicino, prossimo, presso.
nightly: di ogni notte, ogni notte.
nor: ne.
offices: uffici.
owl: gufo, civetta.
quaint: bizzarro, antiquato.
queen: regina.
rest: riposo, riposarsi, riposare, resto, pausa.
sing: cantare, canta, cantano, cantate, canti, cantiamo, canto.

song: canzone, canto.
spell: compitare, sillabare, incantesimo, sortilegio.
spotted: maculato.
sweet: dolce, soave, caramella.

        Beetles black, **approach** not near;
        Worm **nor snail** do no offence.
CHORUS
        Philomel with **melody, etc**.
FIRST FAIRY
        Hence away; now all is well.
        One, **aloof, stand sentinel**.

        [Exeunt FAIRIES. TITANIA sleeps.]

        [Enter OBERON.]
OBERON
        What **thou** seest when thou dost wake,
        [Squeezes the **flower** on TITANIA'S **eyelids**.]
        Do it for **thy** true-love take;
        Love and **languish** for his sake;
        Be it **ounce**, or **cat**, or bear,
        Pard, or **boar** with bristled hair,
        In thy eye that shall appear
        When thou wak'st, it is thy dear;
        Wake when some **vile** thing is near.
        [Exit.]
        [Enter LYSANDER and HERMIA.]
LYSANDER
        Fair love, you **faint** with **wandering** in the wood;
        And, to **speak** troth, I have **forgot** our way;
        We'll **rest** us, Hermia, if you think it good,
        And **tarry** for the **comfort** of the day.
HERMIA
        Be it so, Lysander: find you out a bed,
        For I upon this bank will rest my head.

Italian

aloof: appartato, in disparte, alla larga, a distanza, distante.
approach: accesso, approccio, avvicinare, avvicinamento, avvicinarsi, accostare.
boar: verro.
cat: gatto, il gatto.
comfort: consolare, comodità, confortare, comfort, benessere.
etc: ecc.
eye: occhio, cruna.
faint: debole, svenire, svengo, svengono, sveniamo, svenite, svieni, svenimento, vago.
flower: fiore, fiorire.
forgot: dimenticato.
languish: languire.
melody: melodia.
nor: ne.
ounce: oncia.
rest: riposo, riposarsi, riposare, resto, pausa.
sentinel: sentinella.
snail: chiocciola, lumaca.
speak: parlare, parla, parlo, parliamo, parli, parlate, parlano, favellare.
stand: stare in piedi, granaio, alzarsi, bancarella.
tarry: rimanere, catramoso, rimangono, rimani, rimango, rimanete, rimaniamo.
thou: tu.
thy: tuo.
vile: abietto.
wandering: vagando, peregrinazione.

LYSANDER

One **turf** shall **serve** as **pillow** for us both;
One heart, one bed, two bosoms, and one troth.

HERMIA

Nay, good Lysander; for my **sake**, my dear,
Lie **farther** off yet, do not **lie** so near.

LYSANDER

O, take the sense, **sweet**, of my innocence;
Love **takes** the **meaning** in love's conference.
I mean that my heart **unto yours** is knit;
So that but one heart we can make of it:
Two bosoms interchained with an oath;
So then two bosoms and a **single** troth.
Then by your side no bed-room me deny;
For **lying** so, Hermia, I do not lie.

HERMIA

Lysander riddles very prettily:--
Now much beshrew my **manners** and my pride
If Hermia **meant** to say Lysander lied!
But, **gentle friend**, for love and courtesy
Lie further off; in **human** modesty,
Such **separation** as may well be said
Becomes a **virtuous bachelor** and a maid:
So far be **distant**; and good night, sweet friend:
Thy love ne'er **alter till thy** sweet life end!

LYSANDER

Amen, **amen**, to that fair **prayer** say I;
And then end life when I end loyalty!
Here is my bed: Sleep give **thee** all his rest!

HERMIA

With half that **wish** the wisher's eyes be **pressed**!

Italian

alter: cambiarsi, alterare, altera, alteriamo, alterano, alteri, alterate, altero, modificare, mutare, cambiare.
amen: amen.
bachelor: scapolo, celibe, baccelliere.
distant: distante, lontano.
farther: più lontano.
friend: amico, amica.
gentle: mite, gentile, dolce, delicato.
human: umano.
lie: mentire, bugia, giacere, menzogna
lying: mentire, bugiardo, giacente.

manners: educazione.
meaning: significato, intenzione, accezione, senso.
meant: significato.
pillow: guanciale, cuscino.
prayer: preghiera, orazione.
pressed: premuto.
sake: causa.
separation: separazione, distacco.
serve: servire, serviamo, servi, servono, servite, servo.
single: singolo, celibe, nubile, solo,

single.
sweet: dolce, soave, caramella.
takes: prende.
thee: te.
thy: tuo.
till: finchè, coltivare, cassa, fino, arare.
turf: tappeto erboso, zolla erbosa.
unto: a.
virtuous: virtuoso.
wish: desiderio, volere, desiderare, volontà, voglia.
yours: il vostro, vostro.

[They   sleep.]

[Enter PUCK.]

PUCK

    Through the **forest** have I gone,

    But Athenian found I none,

    On **whose** eyes I might approve

    This flower's **force** in **stirring** love.

    Night and **silence**! Who is here?

    Weeds of Athens he doth wear:

    This is he, my **master** said,

    Despised the Athenian maid;

    And here the **maiden**, **sleeping** sound,

    On the **dank** and **dirty** ground.

    Pretty **soul**! she durst not lie

    Near this lack-love, this **kill**-courtesy.

    Churl, upon **thy** eyes I throw

    All the power this **charm** doth owe;

    When **thou** wak'st let love forbid

    Sleep his **seat** on thy eyelid:

    So **awake** when I am gone;

    For I must now to Oberon.

[Exit.]

[Enter DEMETRIUS and HELENA, running.]

HELENA

    Stay, though thou kill me, **sweet** Demetrius.

DEMETRIUS

    I **charge thee**, **hence**, and do not **haunt** me thus.

HELENA

    O, **wilt** thou darkling **leave** me? do not so.

Italian

awake: sveglio, svegliarsi.

charge: carica, carico, addebito, spese, onere, tassa, caricare, imputazione, accusa.

charm: fascino, incanto.

dank: bagnato, umido.

dirty: sporco, sporcare, imbrattare, insudiciare.

force: forza, forzare, costringere, vigore.

forest: bosco, foresta, selva.

haunt: frequentare.

hence: da qui, quindi.

kill: uccidere, ammazzare.

leave: lasciare, abbandonare, partire, lasciano, partono, partite, partiamo, parti, lasciate, lasciamo, lascia.

maiden: nubile, fanciulla.

master: maestro, padrone, principale, master, dominare, anagrafica.

seat: posto, sede, sedile, seggio, sedia.

silence: silenzio.

sleeping: dormendo, addormentato.

soul: anima.

stirring: mescolare, eccitante, agitazione.

sweet: dolce, soave, caramella.

thee: te.

thou: tu.

thy: tuo.

whose: di chi, il cui.

wilt: appassire, appassisco, appassiscono, appassisci, appassiamo, appassite.

DEMETRIUS.

Stay on **thy peril**; I **alone** will go.

[Exit DEMETRIUS.]

HELENA

O, I am out of **breath** in this **fond** chase!
The more my **prayer**, the **lesser** is my grace.
Happy is Hermia, wheresoe'er she lies,
For she hath **blessed** and **attractive** eyes.
How came her eyes so bright? Not with **salt** tears:
If so, my eyes are oftener wash'd than hers.
No, no, I am as **ugly** as a bear;
For beasts that meet me run away for fear:
Therefore no **marvel** though Demetrius
Do, as a **monster**, fly my presence thus.
What **wicked** and **dissembling glass** of mine
Made me **compare** with Hermia's sphery eyne?--
But who is here?--Lysander! on the ground!
Dead? or **asleep**? I see no **blood**, no wound.
Lysander, if you live, good **sir**, **awake**.

LYSANDER

[Waking.]
And run through **fire** I will for thy sweet sake.
Transparent Helena! **Nature shows** art,
That through thy **bosom makes** me see thy heart.
Where is Demetrius? O, how fit a word
Is that **vile** name to **perish** on my **sword**!

HELENA

Do not say so, Lysander; say not so:
What though he love your Hermia? Lord, what though?
Yet Hermia still **loves** you: then be **content**.

Italian

alone: solo, da solo, solamente.
asleep: addormentato.
attractive: attraente, seducente, allettante, attrattivo, avvenente.
awake: sveglio, svegliarsi.
blessed: benedetto, beato.
blood: sangue.
bosom: petto, seno.
breath: alito, respiro, fiato, soffio.
compare: confrontare, confronta, confrontiamo, confronti, confrontano, confrontate, confronto, paragonare, paragono, paragona, paragonate.

content: contenuto, contento, soddisfatto, soddisfare.
dissembling: dissimulando.
fire: fuoco, incendio, sparare, rogo.
fond: tenero, affettuoso, affezionato.
glass: vetro, bicchiere, cristallo.
lesser: minore.
loves: amore.
makes: fa, commette.
marvel: meraviglia, stupirsi.
monster: mostro.

nature: natura, indole, carattere.
peril: pericolo.
perish: perire.
prayer: preghiera, orazione.
salt: sale, salare, salato, il sale.
shows: mostra.
sir: signore.
sword: spada.
thy: tuo.
ugly: brutto.
vile: abietto.
wicked: cattivo, malvagio.

LYSANDER.

    Content with Hermia? No: I do repent
    The **tedious minutes** I with her have spent.
    Not Hermia but Helena I love:
    Who will not change a **raven** for a dove?
    The will of man is by his **reason** sway'd;
    And reason says you are the worthier maid.
    Things **growing** are not **ripe** until their season;
    So I, being young, **till** now ripe not to reason;
    And **touching** now the point of **human** skill,
    Reason **becomes** the **marshal** to my will,
    And **leads** me to your eyes, where I o'erlook
    Love's stories, **written** in love's richest book.

HELENA

    Wherefore was I to this **keen mockery** born?
    When at your **hands** did I **deserve** this scorn?
    Is't not enough, is't not enough, young man,
    That I did never, no, **nor** never can
    Deserve a **sweet** look from Demetrius' eye,
    But you must **flout** my insufficiency?
    Good troth, you do me wrong,--good sooth, you do--
    In such **disdainful manner** me to woo.
    But **fare** you well: **perforce** I must confess,
    I **thought** you **lord** of more **true** gentleness.
    O, that a **lady** of one man refus'd
    Should of another therefore be abus'd!

    [Exit.]

LYSANDER

    She **sees** not Hermia:--Hermia, **sleep** thou there;
    And never mayst thou come Lysander near!
    For, as a surfeit of the sweetest things

Italian

becomes: diviene, diventa.
deserve: meritare, meritano, merita, meritate, meritiamo, meriti, merito.
disdainful: sdegnoso, sprezzante.
fare: tariffa.
flout: schernire.
growing: crescendo, coltivando.
hands: mani.
human: umano.
keen: aguzzo, acuto, tagliente, affilato.
lady: signora, dama.
leads: conduce, guida.

lord: signore.
manner: maniera, modo.
marshal: schierare, maresciallo.
minutes: verbale, contravvenzione, minuti.
mockery: derisione.
nor: ne.
perforce: necessariamente.
raven: corvo, corvo imperiale, corvino.
reason: ragione, causa, intelletto, ragionare, argomentare, motivo.
ripe: maturo.

sees: vede, sega.
sleep: sonno, dormire, dormi, dormiamo, dormite, dormo, dormono.
sweet: dolce, soave, caramella.
tedious: noioso, tedioso.
thou: tu.
till: finchè, coltivare, cassa, fino, arare.
touching: commovente.
true: vero.
written: scritto.

The   deepest **loathing** to the **stomach** brings;
Or, as the heresies that men do leave
Are **hated** most of those they did deceive;
So **thou**, my surfeit and my heresy,
Of all be hated, but the most of me!
And, all my **powers**, **address** your love and might
To **honour** Helen, and to be her knight!
[Exit.]

HERMIA
[Starting.]
Help me, Lysander, help me! do **thy** best
To **pluck** this crawling **serpent** from my breast!
Ay me, for pity!--What a **dream** was here!
Lysander, look how I do **quake** with fear!
Methought a serpent **eat** my **heart** away,
And you **sat smiling** at his **cruel** prey.--
Lysander! what, **removed**? Lysander! lord!
What, out of **hearing**? **gone**? no **sound**, no word?
Alack, where are you? **speak**, an if you hear;
Speak, of all **loves**! I **swoon** almost with fear.
No?--then I well **perceive** you are not nigh:
Either death or you I'll find immediately.
[Exit.]

Italian

address: indirizzo, indirizzare, recapito, discorso, l'indirizzo.
cruel: crudele.
dream: sogno, sognare.
eat: mangiare, mangi, mangia, mangiamo, mangiano, mangiate, mangio.
gone: andato.
hated: odiato.
hearing: udendo, sentendo, udito, udienza, ascolto.
heart: cuore, il cuore.

honour: onore.
loathing: detestando, ripugnanza.
loves: amore.
perceive: percepire, accorgersi, scorgere, percepiamo, scorgo, scorgiamo, scorgi, scorgete, percepite, scorgono, percepiscono.
pluck: rompere, staccare, cogliere, spennare, strappare, fegato.
powers: poteri.
quake: tremito, tremare.
removed: tolto, asportato, rimosso.

sat: seduto, covato.
serpent: serpente.
smiling: sorridere.
sound: suono, sonare, suonare, solido, sondare, sano, scandagliare, rumore, sonda.
speak: parlare, parla, parlo, parliamo, parli, parlate, parlano, favellare.
stomach: stomaco, ventre.
swoon: svenire, deliquio, svenimento.
thou: tu.
thy: tuo.

ACT III

SCENE I. THE WOOD. THE QUEEN OF FAIRIES LYING ASLEEP.

[Enter QUINCE, SNUG, BOTTOM, FLUTE, SNOUT, and STARVELING.]

BOTTOM

Are we all **met**?

QUINCE

Pat, **pat**; and here's a **marvellous convenient** place for our **rehearsal**. This **green plot** shall be our **stage**, this **hawthorn brake** our tiring-house; and we will do it in action, as we will do it before the **duke**.

BOTTOM

Peter Quince,--

QUINCE

What sayest **thou, bully** Bottom?

BOTTOM

There are things in this **comedy** of 'Pyramus and Thisby' that will never **please**. First, Pyramus must **draw** a **sword** to **kill** himself; which the **ladies cannot abide**. How **answer** you that?

Italian

abide: aspettare, aspettiamo, aspetta, aspettano, aspetti, aspetto, aspettate, restare, sopportare.
answer: risposta, rispondere, replicare, rispondere a.
brake: freno, frenare.
bully: prepotente.
cannot: non potere.
comedy: commedia.
convenient: conveniente.
draw: disegnare, disegna, disegniamo, disegni, disegnate, disegnano,

disegno, tirare, attrarre, sorteggio, eguaglianza.
duke: duca.
green: verde, acerbo.
hawthorn: biancospino.
kill: uccidere, ammazzare.
ladies: signore.
marvellous: meraviglioso.
met: incontrato.
pat: colpetto.
please: piacere, per favore, per piacere, prego.

plot: complotto, trama, macchinare, complottare, appezzamento, intreccio, congiura, disegnare.
rehearsal: prova.
stage: palcoscenico, fase, stadio, scena, palco.
sword: spada.
thou: tu.

SNOUT

By'r lakin, a parlous **fear**.

STARVELING

I believe we must leave the **killing** out, when all is done.

BOTTOM

Not a **whit**: I have a **device** to make all well. **Write** me a **prologue**; and let the prologue **seem** to say we will do no harm with our swords, and that Pyramus is not **killed indeed**; and for the more better **assurance**, tell them that I Pyramus am not Pyramus but Bottom the **weaver**: this will put them out of fear.

QUINCE

Well, we will have such a prologue; and it shall be written in **eight** and six.

BOTTOM

No, make it two more; let it be written in eight and eight.

SNOUT

Will not the ladies be afeard of the lion?

STARVELING

I fear it, I promise you.

BOTTOM

Masters, you **ought** to **consider** with **yourselves**: to bring in, God **shield** us! a lion among ladies is a most **dreadful** thing: for there is not a more **fearful** wild-fowl than your lion **living**; and we ought to look to it.

SNOUT

Therefore another prologue must tell he is not a lion.

BOTTOM

Nay, you must name his name, and half his face must be seen through the lion's **neck**; and he himself must speak through, **saying** thus, or to the same defect,--'Ladies,' or, 'Fair ladies, I would wish you, or, I would request you, or, I would **entreat** you, not to fear, not to **tremble**: my life for yours. If you think I come **hither** as a lion, it were **pity** of my life. No, I am no such thing; I

Italian

assurance: assicurazione, promessa.
consider: considerare, consideri, considerano, consideriamo, considera, considerate, considero, guardare.
device: dispositivo, apparecchio, congegno.
dreadful: terribile.
eight: otto.
entreat: supplicare.
fear: paura, temere, angoscia, timore, aver timore.

fearful: spaventoso, pauroso.
hither: qui, quà.
indeed: davvero, infatti, di fatto, veramente.
killed: ucciso.
killing: uccisione.
living: vivendo, abitando, vivo, vivente.
neck: collo, pomiciare, il collo.
ought: dovere.
pity: compassione, pietà.
prologue: prologo.

saying: dicendo, detto, proverbio.
seem: parere, paiono, paiamo, pari, paio, parete, sembrare, sembra, sembrano, sembrate, sembri.
shield: scudo, riparo, proteggere, schermo, schermare.
tremble: tremare.
weaver: tessitore.
whit: briciolo.
write: scrivere, scrivi, scrivono, scriviamo, scrivete, scrivo.
yourselves: voi stessi.

am a man as other men are:'--and there, indeed, let him name his name, and
tell them plainly he is Snug the joiner.

QUINCE

Well, it shall be so. But there is two hard things; that is, to bring the
moonlight into a **chamber**: for, you know, Pyramus and Thisbe meet by
moonlight.

SNOUT

Doth the moon **shine** that night we play our play?

BOTTOM

A **calendar**, a calendar! look in the almanack; find out **moonshine**, find out
moonshine.

QUINCE

Yes, it doth shine that night.

BOTTOM

Why, then may you leave a casement of the great chamber-window, where
we play, open; and the moon may shine in at the casement.

QUINCE

Ay; or else one must come in with a **bush** of thorns and a **lantern**, and say he
comes to **disfigure** or to **present** the **person** of moonshine. Then there is
another thing: we must have a **wall** in the great chamber; for Pyramus and
Thisby, says the story, did **talk** through the **chink** of a wall.

SNOUT

You can never bring in a wall.--What say you, Bottom?

BOTTOM

Some man or other must present wall: and let him have some **plaster**, or
some **loam**, or some rough-cast about him, to **signify** wall; and let him hold
his **fingers** thus, and through that **cranny** shall Pyramus and Thisby **whisper**.

QUINCE

If that may be, then all is well. Come, **sit** down, every mother's son, and

---

Italian

bush: arbusto, cespuglio, boccola, bussola.
calendar: calendario.
chamber: camera.
chink: fessura.
cranny: fessura, crepa.
disfigure: sfigurare, sfiguriamo, sfiguri, sfiguro, sfigurate, sfigurano, sfigura.
fingers: dito.
lantern: lanterna.
loam: argilla.

moon: luna, la luna.
moonlight: chiaro di luna.
moonshine: chiaro di luna.
plaster: intonaco, intonacare, cerotto, gesso.
present: presente, regalo, dono, presentare, attuale.
shine: risplendere, brillare, lustro, splendere.
signify: significare, significate, significo, significhi, significa, significhiamo, significano.

sit: sedere, sediamo, siedono, siedi, sedete, siedo, covare, covo, covi, cova, covate.
son: figlio, figliolo, il figlio.
talk: parlare, parlo, parliamo, parli, parlate, parlano, parla, discorso, discorrere, conversazione, conversare.
wall: muro, parete.
whisper: sussurrare, bisbigliare, bisbiglio.

rehearse your parts. Pyramus, you **begin**: when you have **spoken** your **speech**, enter into that **brake**; and so every one **according** to his cue.

[Enter PUCK behind.]

PUCK

What **hempen** homespuns have we swaggering here,
So near the **cradle** of the **fairy** queen?
What, a play **toward**! I'll be an auditor;
An **actor** too perhaps, if I see **cause**.

QUINCE

Speak, Pyramus.--Thisby, stand **forth**.

PYRAMUS

'Thisby, the flowers of **odious** savours sweet,'

QUINCE

Odours, odours.

PYRAMUS

'--odours savours sweet:
So hath **thy breath**, my dearest Thisby dear.--
But **hark**, a voice! stay **thou** but here awhile,
And by and by I will to **thee** appear.'

[Exit.]

PUCK

A **stranger** Pyramus than e'er **played** here!

[Aside.--Exit.]

THISBE

Must I speak now?

QUINCE

Ay, **marry**, must you: for you must **understand** he goes
but to see a **noise** that he heard, and is to come again.

Italian

according: secondo.
actor: attore.
begin: cominciare, cominci, cominciate, cominciano, comincia, cominciamo, comincio, iniziare, inizi, iniziate, iniziano.
brake: freno, frenare.
breath: alito, respiro, fiato, soffio.
cause: causa, causare, provocare.
cradle: culla, luogo d'origine, cullare.
fairy: fata.
forth: avanti.

hark: ascoltare.
hempen: di canapa.
marry: sposare, sposati, sposatevi, si sposi, si sposate, si sposano, ci sposiamo, mi sposo, maritarsi, ammogliarsi, maritare.
noise: rumore, schiamazzo.
odious: odioso.
played: giocato, suonato.
rehearse: proviamo, provo, provi, provate, provano, provare, prova.
speech: discorso, orazione, parola.

spoken: parlato.
stranger: sconosciuto, estraneo, forestiero.
thee: te.
thou: tu.
thy: tuo.
toward: verso, a.
understand: capire, capite, capiamo, capisci, capisco, capiscono, comprendere, comprendono, comprendo, comprendiamo, comprendete.

THISBE

'Most radiant Pyramus, most **lily** white of hue,
Of **colour** like the **red rose** on **triumphant** brier,
Most brisky juvenal, and eke most **lovely** Jew,
As true as truest horse, that would never tire,
I'll meet **thee**, Pyramus, at Ninny's **tomb**.'

QUINCE

Ninus' tomb, man: why, you must not speak that yet:
that you answer to Pyramus. You speak all your part at once,
cues, and all.--Pyramus **enter**: your cue is past; it is 'never
tire.'

[Re-enter PUCK, and BOTTOM with an ass's head.]

THISBE

O,'--As true as truest horse, that yet would never tire.'

PYRAMUS

'If I were **fair**, Thisby, I were only thine:--'

QUINCE

O **monstrous**! O **strange**! we are **haunted**. **Pray**, masters!
fly, masters! Help!

[Exeunt Clowns.]

PUCK

I'll follow you; I'll lead you about a round,
Through **bog**, through **bush**, through **brake**, through brier;
Sometime a horse I'll be, sometime a **hound**,
A **hog**, a **headless bear**, sometime a fire;
And **neigh**, and **bark**, and **grunt**, and **roar**, and burn,
Like horse, hound, hog, bear, fire, at every turn.
[Exit.]

BOTTOM

Why do they run away? This is a **knavery** of them to make me afeard.

Italian

bark: corteccia, abbaiare, scorza, latrare, abbaio.
bear: orso, produrre, ribassista, partorire, l'orso, portare.
bog: palude, acquitrino, pantano.
brake: freno, frenare.
bush: arbusto, cespuglio, boccola, bussola.
colour: colore.
cue: stecca.
enter: entrare, entra, entrano, entrate, entri, entriamo, entro, invio.

fair: biondo, fiera, giusto, bazar, correttamente, bello, equo.
grunt: grugnito, grugnire.
haunted: frequentato, perseguitato.
headless: senza testa.
hog: porco, maiale.
hound: cane da caccia.
knavery: bricconeria.
lily: giglio.
lovely: bello, piacevole, amabile, grazioso, gradevole, affascinante, caro, carino.

monstrous: mostruoso.
neigh: nitrire, nitrito.
pray: pregare, pregate, prego, preghi, prega, preghiamo, pregano.
red: rosso.
roar: ruggire, muggire, ruggito, scrosciare.
rose: rosa.
strange: strano.
thee: te.
tomb: tomba, sepolcro.
triumphant: trionfante.

[Re-enter SNOUT.]

SNOUT

O Bottom, **thou** art changed! What do I see on **thee**?

BOTTOM

What do you see? you see an **ass**-head of your own, do you?

[Re-enter QUINCE.]

QUINCE

Bless thee, Bottom! **bless** thee! thou art translated.

[Exit.]

BOTTOM

I see their **knavery**: this is to make an ass of me; to **fright** me, if they could. But I will not **stir** from this place, do what they can: I will **walk** up and down here, and I will **sing**, that they shall **hear** I am not afraid.

[Sings.]

The ousel **cock**, so black of hue,

With orange-tawny bill,

The throstle **with** his **note** so true,

The **wren** with little **quill**.

TITANIA

[Waking.]

What **angel** wakes me from my **flowery** bed?

BOTTOM

[Sings.]

The **finch**, the **sparrow**, and the lark,

The plain-song **cuckoo** gray,

Whose note full many a man doth mark,

And **dares** not answer nay;--

for, indeed, who would set his wit to so **foolish** a **bird**?

Who would give a bird the **lie**, though he **cry** 'cuckoo' never so?

Italian

angel: angelo.
ass: asino, ciuco, somaro, culo.
bird: uccello, l'uccello.
bless: benedire, benedi', benedite, benedicono, benedico, benedici, benediciamo.
cock: gallo, cazzo, rubinetto.
cry: piangere, grido, gridare, urlare.
cuckoo: cuculo.
dares: osa.
finch: fringuello.
flowery: fiorito.

foolish: sciocco, stupido, stolto, ignorante, fesso.
fright: paura, spavento, timore, angoscia.
hear: udire, odono, odi, odo, udite, udiamo, sentire, sentono, sento, sentite, senti.
knavery: bricconeria.
lie: mentire, bugia, giacere, menzogna.
note: nota, biglietto, appunto, annotazione, notare, annotare.
quill: penna d'oca.

sing: cantare, canta, cantano, cantate, canti, cantiamo, canto.
sparrow: passero.
stir: mescolare, agitare, muovere.
thee: te.
thou: tu.
walk: camminare, cammino, cammina, camminano, camminate, cammini, camminiamo, camminata, passeggiare, passeggiata.
wit: arguzia.
wren: scricciolo.

A Midsummer Night's Dream

TITANIA

I pray **thee**, gentle **mortal**, sing again;
Mine ear is much enamour'd of **thy** note.
So is mine eye **enthralled** to thy shape;
And thy fair virtue's force **perforce** doth move me,
On the first view, to say, to swear, I love thee.

BOTTOM

Methinks, mistress, you should have little reason for
that: and yet, to say the **truth**, reason and love keep little
company together now-a-days: the more the pity that some honest
neighbours will not make them friends. **Nay**, I can gleek upon
occasion.

TITANIA

Thou art as **wise** as **thou** art **beautiful**.

BOTTOM

Not so, **neither**: but if I had wit enough to get out of
this wood, I have enough to serve mine own turn.

TITANIA

Out of this wood do not desire to go;
Thou shalt **remain** here whether thou **wilt** or no.
I am a spirit of no **common** rate,--
The **summer** still doth **tend** upon my state;
And I do love thee: therefore, go with me,
I'll give thee fairies to **attend** on thee;
And they shall fetch thee jewels from the deep,
And sing, while thou on pressed flowers dost sleep:
And I will **purge** thy mortal **grossness** so
That thou shalt like an **airy** spirit go.--
Peasblossom! **Cobweb! Moth!** and Mustardseed!
[Enter Four FAIRIES.]

Italian

airy: arioso.
attend: visitare, curare, assistere, curiamo, curi, curo, curano, visitate, visitiamo, cura, visiti.
beautiful: bello, carino, bella, bellissimo.
cobweb: ragnatela.
common: comune, volgare, ordinario.
enthralled: affascinato.
grossness: grossezza, volgarità, grossolanità.
mortal: mortale.

moth: falena, tarma, tignola.
nay: anzi.
neither: ne, neanche, nemmeno, neppure.
perforce: necessariamente.
purge: epurazione, purgare, pulire, purga, spurgo, epurare, eliminare, purgante.
remain: rimanere, rimangono, rimani, rimango, rimanete, rimaniamo, restare, restiamo, resti, restate, restano.

summer: estate, l'estate.
tend: tendere, prendersi cura di, tendete, tendi, tendiamo, tendo, tendono.
thee: te.
thou: tu.
thy: tuo.
truth: verità.
wilt: appassire, appassisco, appassiscono, appassisci, appassiamo, appassite.
wise: saggio, assennato.

FIRST FAIRY
  Ready.
SECOND FAIRY
      And I.
THIRD FAIRY
        And I.
FOURTH FAIRY
            Where shall we go?
TITANIA
  Be kind and **courteous** to this gentleman;
  Hop in his **walks** and **gambol** in his eyes;
  Feed him with apricocks and dewberries,
  With **purple grapes**, **green figs**, and mulberries;
  The **honey bags steal** from the humble-bees,
  And, for night-tapers, **crop** their **waxen** thighs,
  And **light** them at the **fiery** glow-worm's eyes,
  To have my love to **bed** and to arise;
  And **pluck** the **wings** from **painted** butterflies,
  To **fan** the moonbeams from his **sleeping** eyes:
  Nod to him, elves, and do him courtesies.
FIRST FAIRY
  Hail, **mortal**!
SECOND FAIRY
  Hail!
THIRD FAIRY
  Hail!
FOURTH FAIRY
  Hail!
BOTTOM
  I **cry** your worships **mercy**, heartily.--I **beseech** your worship's name.

Italian

bags: borse.
bed: letto, il letto.
beseech: supplicare, scongiurare,
  implorare.
courteous: cortese.
crop: raccolto.
cry: piangere, grido, gridare, urlare.
fan: ventilatore, ventola, tifoso,
  ventaglio, ammiratore.
fiery: infuocato.
figs: fichi.
fourth: quarto, quarta.

gambol: capriola.
grapes: uva.
green: verde, acerbo.
honey: miele.
light: luce, leggero, accendere, chiaro,
  illuminare, fanale, lampada,
  luminoso, debole.
mercy: misericordia.
mortal: mortale.
painted: dipinto, verniciato.
pluck: rompere, staccare, cogliere,
  spennare, strappare, fegato.

purple: viola, porpora, rosso porpora.
sleeping: dormendo, addormentato.
steal: rubare.
walks: cammina.
waxen: cereo.
wings: diritti d'acquisto di titoli
  negoziabili del Governo.

COBWEB

Cobweb.

BOTTOM

I shall **desire** you of more **acquaintance**, good Master Cobweb. If I cut my **finger**, I shall make **bold** with you.--Your name, **honest gentleman**?

PEASBLOSSOM

Peasblossom.

BOTTOM

I **pray** you, **commend** me to Mistress Squash, your mother, and to Master Peascod, your father. Good Master Peasblossom, I shall desire you of more acquaintance too.--Your name, I **beseech** you, sir?

MUSTARDSEED

Mustardseed.

BOTTOM

Good Master Mustardseed, I know your **patience** well: That same **cowardly** giant-like ox-beef hath **devoured** many a gentleman of your house: I **promise** you your **kindred** hath made my eyes water ere now. I desire you of more acquaintance, good Master Mustardseed.

TITANIA

Come, **wait** upon him; **lead** him to my **bower**.
The **moon**, methinks, **looks** with a **watery** eye;
And when she **weeps**, weeps every little flower;
Lamenting some enforcèd chastity.
Tie up my love's **tongue**, bring him **silently**.

[Exeunt.]

SCENE II. ANOTHER PART OF THE WOOD.

Italian

acquaintance: conoscenza, conoscente.
beseech: supplicare, scongiurare, implorare.
bold: grassetto, spesso, grosso, audace.
bower: ancora di prora, pergolato.
commend: lodare, loda, lodiamo, lodo, lodi, lodate, lodano, raccomandare, vantare.
cowardly: vigliacco, codardo.
desire: desiderio, desiderare, bramare.
devoured: divorato.

finger: dito, il dito.
gentleman: signore, galantuomo, gentiluomo.
honest: onesto.
kindred: parentela, affine.
lead: piombo, condurre, conduciamo, conducono, conduco, conducete, conduci, guidare, guidiamo, guidano, guidate.
looks: guarda.
moon: luna, la luna.
patience: pazienza.

pray: pregare, pregate, prego, preghi, prega, preghiamo, pregano.
promise: promessa, promettere, promettono, promettete, prometti, promettiamo, prometto.
silently: silenziosamente.
tongue: lingua, linguetta, la lingua.
wait: aspettare, aspetto, aspetta, aspettano, aspettate, aspetti, aspettiamo, attesa.
watery: acquoso.
weeps: piange.

[Enter OBERON.]

OBERON

    I **wonder** if Titania be awak'd;

    Then, what it was that next came in her eye,

    Which she must **dote** on in extremity.

    [Enter PUCK.]

    Here comes my messenger.--How now, **mad** spirit?

    What night-rule now about this **haunted grove**?

PUCK

    My **mistress** with a monster is in love.

    Near to her **close** and consecrated bower,

    While she was in her **dull** and sleeping hour,

    A **crew** of **patches**, **rude** mechanicals,

    That work for **bread** upon Athenian stalls,

    Were met together to **rehearse** a play

    Intended for great Theseus' **nuptial** day.

    The shallowest thickskin of that **barren** sort

    Who Pyramus **presented** in their sport,

    Forsook his **scene** and enter'd in a brake;

    When I did him at this **advantage** take,

    An ass's nowl I fixèd on his head;

    Anon, his Thisbe must be answered,

    And forth my **mimic** comes. When they him spy,

    As wild **geese** that the **creeping fowler** eye,

    Or russet-pated choughs, many in sort,

    Rising and cawing at the gun's report,

    Sever themselves and **madly sweep** the sky,

    So at his sight away his fellows fly:

    And at our **stamp** here, o'er and o'er one falls;

    He **murder** cries, and help from Athens calls.

    Their sense thus **weak**, **lost** with their fears, thus strong,

Italian

advantage: vantaggio, beneficio, guadagno, profitto.
barren: sterile.
bread: pane, impanare, il pane.
close: chiudere, vicino, chiudo, chiudono, chiudiamo, chiudete, chiudi, prossimo, chiuso.
creeping: strisciando, strisciante.
crew: equipaggio, squadra.
dote: essere rimbambito.
dull: opaco, smussato, spuntato.
fowler: uccellatore.

geese: oche.
grove: boschetto.
haunted: frequentato, perseguitato.
lost: perso, perduto, smarrito.
mad: matto, pazzo, arrabbiato, rabbioso, folle.
madly: pazzamente, follemente.
mimic: imitare, mimetico, imitativo.
mistress: padrona.
murder: omicidio, assassinare, assassinio.
nuptial: nuziale.

patches: toppe.
presented: presentato.
rehearse: proviamo, provo, provi, provate, provano, provare, prova.
rude: scortese, rozzo, maleducato.
scene: scena.
stamp: francobollo, bollo, bollare, timbro, affrancare, timbrare.
sweep: spazzare, scopare, spazzata.
weak: debole, fiacco.
wonder: stupirsi, stupore, meraviglia, domandarsi, meravigliarsi.

Made **senseless** things **begin** to do them wrong;
For briers and thorns at their **apparel** snatch;
Some **sleeves**, some hats: from yielders all things catch.
I **led** them on in this **distracted fear**,
And left **sweet** Pyramus **translated** there:
When in that moment,--so it came to pass,--
Titania wak'd, and straightway lov'd an ass.

OBERON

This **falls** out better than I could devise.
But hast **thou** yet latch'd the Athenian's eyes
With the love-juice, as I did **bid thee** do?

PUCK

I took him sleeping,--that is finish'd too,--
And the Athenian woman by his side;
That, when he wak'd, of force she must be ey'd.

[**Enter** DEMETRIUS and HERMIA.]

OBERON

Stand close; this is the same Athenian.

PUCK

This is the woman, but not this the man.

DEMETRIUS

O, why **rebuke** you him that **loves** you so?
Lay **breath** so **bitter** on your bitter **foe**.

HERMIA

Now I but **chide**, but I should use thee worse;
For thou, I fear, hast given me **cause** to curse.
If thou hast **slain** Lysander in his sleep,
Being o'er **shoes** in **blood**, **plunge** in the deep,
And **kill** me too.
The **sun** was not so true **unto** the day

Italian

apparel: vestimento, abito.
begin: cominciare, cominci, cominciate, cominciano, comincia, cominciamo, comincio, iniziare, inizi, iniziate, iniziano.
bid: offerta, offrire, chiedere.
bitter: amaro.
blood: sangue.
breath: alito, respiro, fiato, soffio.
cause: causa, causare, provocare.
chide: sgrida, sgrido, sgridiamo, sgridi, sgridano, sgridate, sgridare.

distracted: distratto.
enter: entrare, entra, entrano, entrate, entri, entriamo, entro, invio.
falls: cade.
fear: paura, temere, angoscia, timore, aver timore.
foe: nemico.
kill: uccidere, ammazzare.
led: condotto, guidato.
loves: amore.
plunge: tuffarsi, immergere, tuffare, immersione.

rebuke: biasimare, disapprovare, riprendere, sgridare, rimproverare.
senseless: insensato.
shoes: scarpe.
slain: ucciso, ammazzato.
sleeves: manicotti.
sun: sole.
sweet: dolce, soave, caramella.
thee: te.
thou: tu.
translated: tradotto.
unto: a.

As he to me: would he have stol'n away
From **sleeping** Hermia? I'll believe as soon
This whole earth may be bor'd; and that the moon
May through the centre **creep** and so displease
Her brother's noontide with the antipodes.
It **cannot** be but **thou** hast murder'd him;
So should a **murderer** look; so **dead**, so grim.

DEMETRIUS

So should the murder'd look; and so should I,
Pierc'd through the **heart** with your **stern** cruelty:
Yet you, the murderer, look as **bright**, as clear,
As **yonder** Venus in her glimmering **sphere**.

HERMIA

What's this to my Lysander? where is he?
Ah, good Demetrius, **wilt** thou give him me?

DEMETRIUS

I had rather give his **carcass** to my hounds.

HERMIA

Out, **dog**! out, **cur**! thou driv'st me past the bounds
Of maiden's **patience**. Hast thou **slain** him, then?
Henceforth be never number'd among men!
Oh! once tell **true**; tell true, even for my sake;
Durst thou have look'd upon him, being awake,
And hast thou kill'd him sleeping? O **brave** touch!
Could not a **worm**, an **adder**, do so much?
An adder did it; for with doubler tongue
Than **thine**, thou **serpent**, never adder stung.

DEMETRIUS

You **spend** your **passion** on a mispris'd mood:
I am not **guilty** of Lysander's blood;
Nor is he dead, for aught that I can tell.

Italian

adder: vipera.
brave: coraggioso, valoroso, strenuo, affrontare.
bright: brillante, luminoso, splendente, chiaro.
cannot: non potere.
carcass: carcassa.
creep: strisciare, strisci, strisciamo, strisciano, strisciate, strisciamento, striscia, striscio.
cur: cagnaccio.
dead: morto.

dog: cane, il cane.
guilty: colpevole.
heart: cuore, il cuore.
murderer: assassino.
passion: ardore, passione.
patience: pazienza.
serpent: serpente.
slain: ucciso, ammazzato.
sleeping: dormendo, addormentato.
spend: spendere, spendiamo, spendo, spendi, spendete, spendono, passare, passo, passiamo, passi, passate.

sphere: sfera.
stern: poppa, severo.
thine: le tue, la tua, i tuoi, il tuo.
thou: tu.
true: vero.
wilt: appassire, appassisco, appassiscono, appassisci, appassiamo, appassite.
worm: verme, vite senza fine, lombrico, baco.
yonder: là, laggiù.

HERMIA
   I **pray thee**, tell me, then, that he is well.

DEMETRIUS
   An if I could, what should I get therefore?

HERMIA
   A **privilege** never to see me more.--
   And from **thy hated presence** part I so:
   See me no more whether he be dead or no.
   [Exit.]

DEMETRIUS
   There is no following her in this **fierce** vein:
   Here, therefore, for a while I will remain.
   So **sorrow's heaviness** doth **heavier** grow
   For **debt** that **bankrupt sleep** doth sorrow owe;
   Which now in some **slight measure** it will pay,
   If for his **tender** here I make some stay.
   [Lies down.]

OBERON
   What hast **thou** done? thou hast **mistaken** quite,
   And **laid** the love-juice on some true-love's sight:
   Of thy misprision must **perforce** ensue
   Some true love turn'd, and not a **false** turn'd true.

PUCK
   Then **fate** o'er-rules, that, one man **holding** troth,
   A million **fail, confounding oath** on oath.

OBERON
   About the **wood** go, swifter than the wind,
   And Helena of Athens look thou find:
   All fancy-sick she is, and **pale** of cheer,
   With sighs of love, that **costs** the **fresh** blood dear.

Italian

bankrupt: fallito, bancarotta, fallimento.
confounding: confondendo.
costs: costo, costi.
debt: debito.
fail: fallire, morire, mancare.
false: falso, finto.
fate: destino, fato, sorte.
fierce: feroce.
fresh: fresco.
hated: odiato.
heavier: più pesante.

heaviness: pesantezza.
holding: tenere, tenuta, detenzione, podere, presa.
laid: posato.
measure: misura, misurare, provvedimento.
mistaken: sbagliato.
oath: giuramento, imprecazione.
pale: pallido, smorto, impallidire.
perforce: necessariamente.
pray: pregare, pregate, prego, preghi, prega, preghiamo, pregano.

presence: presenza.
privilege: privilegio, privilegiare.
sleep: sonno, dormire, dormi, dormiamo, dormite, dormo, dormono.
slight: leggero, lieve.
sorrow: tristezza, cordoglio.
tender: tenero, dolce, offerta, tender.
thee: te.
thou: tu.
thy: tuo.
wood: legno, bosco, selva, legna.

By some **illusion** see **thou bring** her here;
I'll **charm** his eyes against she do appear.

PUCK

I go, I go; look how I go,--
Swifter than **arrow** from the Tartar's bow.
[Exit.]

OBERON

Flower of this **purple** dye,
Hit with Cupid's archery,
Sink in **apple** of his eye!
When his love he doth espy,
Let her **shine** as gloriously
As the Venus of the sky.--
When thou wak'st, if she be by,
Beg of her for **remedy**.

[Re-enter PUCK.]

PUCK

Captain of our **fairy** band,
Helena is here at hand,
And the **youth** mistook by me
Pleading for a lover's fee;
Shall we their **fond** pageant see?
Lord, what fools these mortals be!

OBERON

Stand **aside**: the **noise** they make
Will **cause** Demetrius to **awake**.

PUCK

Then will two at once woo one,--
That must **needs** be **sport** alone;

Italian

apple: mela, la mela.
arrow: freccia, saetta.
aside: da parte, a parte.
awake: sveglio, svegliarsi.
bring: portare, portiamo, porti,
  portano, portate, porto, porta.
cause: causa, causare, provocare.
charm: fascino, incanto.
fairy: fata.
fond: tenero, affettuoso, affezionato.
illusion: illusione.
needs: necessità, bisogno.

noise: rumore, schiamazzo.
purple: viola, porpora, rosso porpora.
remedy: rimedio, medicina, rimediare.
shine: risplendere, brillare, lustro,
  splendere.
sport: sport.
thou: tu.
youth: gioventù, giovinezza,
  adolescenza, giovane.

And those things do best please me
That **befall** preposterously.

[Enter LYSANDER and HELENA.]

LYSANDER

Why should you think that I should woo in **scorn**?
Scorn and **derision** never come in tears.
Look when I **vow**, I **weep**; and vows so born,
In their **nativity** all truth appears.
How can these things in me seem scorn to you,
Bearing the **badge** of faith, to prove them true?

HELENA

You do **advance** your **cunning** more and more.
When truth kills truth, O devilish-holy fray!
These vows are Hermia's: will you give her o'er?
Weigh **oath** with oath, and you will nothing **weigh**:
Your vows to her and me, put in two scales,
Will even weigh; and both as light as tales.

LYSANDER

I had no judgment when to her I swore.

HELENA

Nor none, in my mind, now you give her o'er.

LYSANDER

Demetrius **loves** her, and he loves not you.

DEMETRIUS

[Awaking.]
O Helen, **goddess**, **nymph**, perfect, divine!
To what, my love, shall I **compare thine** eyne?
Crystal is **muddy**. O, how **ripe** in show
Thy lips, those **kissing cherries**, **tempting** grow!
That **pure congealed** white, high Taurus' snow,

Italian

advance: avanzare, anticipo, proporre, avvicinarsi, anticipazione, avanzamento, avanzata, acconto, progredire, prestito, progresso.
badge: distintivo, badge.
befall: succedete, succedi, succediamo, succedo, succedono, succedere.
cherries: ciliege.
compare: confrontare, confronta, confrontiamo, confronti, confrontano, confrontate, confronto, paragonare, paragono, paragona, paragonate.

congealed: congelato.
cunning: astuzia, astuto, furbo.
derision: derisione.
goddess: dea.
kissing: baciare.
loves: amore.
muddy: fangoso, torbido.
nativity: natività.
nymph: ninfa.
oath: giuramento, imprecazione.
pure: puro.
ripe: maturo.

scorn: disprezzo, disprezzare.
tempting: allettante, tentando.
thine: le tue, la tua, i tuoi, il tuo.
vow: voto.
weep: piangere, piangete, piangi, piangiamo, piangono, piango, lacrimare.
weigh: pesare, peso, pesiamo, pesi, pesate, pesa, pesano.

Fann'd with the **eastern wind**, **turns** to a crow
When thou hold'st up thy hand: O, let me kiss
This **princess** of pure white, this **seal** of **bliss**!

HELENA

O **spite**! O hell! I see you all are bent
To set against me for your merriment.
If you were civil, and knew courtesy,
You would not do me thus much injury.
Can you not hate me, as I know you do,
But you must **join** in souls to **mock** me too?
If you were men, as men you are in show,
You would not use a gentle lady so;
To **vow**, and swear, and superpraise my parts,
When I am **sure** you hate me with your hearts.
You both are rivals, and love Hermia;
And now both rivals, to mock Helena:
A **trim exploit**, a **manly** enterprise,
To **conjure** tears up in a **poor** maid's eyes
With your **derision**! **None** of noble sort
Would so **offend** a virgin, and extort
A poor soul's patience, all to make you sport.

LYSANDER

You are **unkind**, Demetrius; be not so;
For you love Hermia: this you know I know:
And here, with all good will, with all my heart,
In Hermia's love I yield you up my part;
And yours of Helena to me bequeath,
Whom I do love and will do till my death.

HELENA

Never did mockers **waste** more **idle** breath.

Italian

bliss: felicità, beatitudine.
conjure: evochiamo, evochi, evoca, evocate, evoco, evocano, fare incantesimi, evocare.
derision: derisione.
eastern: orientale.
exploit: sfruttare, utilizzare, exploit, impresa.
idle: ozioso, pigro, folle, inattivo.
join: congiungere, congiungi, congiungiamo, congiungo, congiungono, congiungete, legare,

unirsi, lego, lega, legano.
manly: virile.
mock: deridere, deridono, derido, deridiamo, deridi, deridete, finto, beffare.
none: nessuno.
offend: offendere, offendiamo, offendo, offendi, offendete, offendono, insultare, insulto, insulti, insultate, insultano.
poor: povero, cattivo.
princess: principessa.

seal: foca, sigillo, la foca, sigillare.
spite: dispetto.
sure: certo, sicuro.
trim: rifilare.
turns: gira, svolta, cambia.
unkind: brusco, rude, scortese.
vow: voto.
waste: spreco, rifiuto, scarto, sprecare, sperperare, rifiuti, sprechi, sprechiamo, sprecate, sprecano, spreca.
wind: vento, flatulenza, avvolgere.

DEMETRIUS

Lysander, keep **thy** Hermia; I will none:
If e'er I lov'd her, all that love is gone.
My **heart** to her but as guest-wise sojourn'd;
And now to Helen is it home return'd,
There to remain.

LYSANDER

Helen, it is not so.

DEMETRIUS

Disparage not the **faith thou** dost not know,
Lest, to thy **peril**, thou aby it **dear**.--
Look where thy love comes; **yonder** is thy dear.

[**Enter** HERMIA.]

HERMIA

Dark night, that from the **eye** his **function** takes,
The ear more **quick** of **apprehension** makes;
Wherein it doth **impair** the **seeing** sense,
It **pays** the **hearing double** recompense:--
Thou art not by **mine** eye, Lysander, found;
Mine ear, I **thank** it, brought me to thy sound.
But why unkindly didst thou leave me so?

LYSANDER

Why should he **stay** whom love doth press to go?

HERMIA

What love could press Lysander from my side?

LYSANDER

Lysander's love, that would not let him bide,--
Fair Helena,--who more engilds the night
Than all yon **fiery** oes and eyes of light.

Italian

apprehension: apprensione, arresto.
dear: caro, costoso, egregio.
double: doppio, sosia, raddoppiare, duplice.
ear: orecchio, spiga, l'orecchio, pannocchia.
enter: entrare, entra, entrano, entrate, entri, entriamo, entro, invio.
eye: occhio, cruna.
faith: fede, fiducia.
fiery: infuocato.
function: funzione, impiego,
funzionare, mansione.
hearing: udendo, sentendo, udito, udienza, ascolto.
impair: danneggiare, danneggiano, danneggiate, danneggio, danneggi, danneggia, danneggiamo.
mine: miniera, mina, minare, estrarre.
pays: paga.
peril: pericolo.
quick: rapido, svelto, veloce.
seeing: vedendo, segando.
stay: stare, sta', stanno, sto, state,
stiamo, stai, restare, rimanere, soggiorno, resta.
thank: ringraziare, ringraziano, ringraziate, ringraziamo, ringrazia, ringrazi, ringrazio.
thou: tu.
thy: tuo.
yon: laggiù, là, li.
yonder: là, laggiù.

Why seek'st **thou** me? could not this make **thee** know
The **hate** I **bare** thee made me leave thee so?

HERMIA

You speak not as you think; it **cannot** be.

HELENA

Lo, she is one of this confederacy!
Now I **perceive** they have conjoin'd all three
To **fashion** this **false** sport in **spite** of me.
Injurious Hermia! most **ungrateful** maid!
Have you conspir'd, have you with these contriv'd,
To **bait** me with this **foul** derision?
Is all the **counsel** that we two have shar'd,
The sisters' vows, the **hours** that we have spent,
When we have chid the hasty-footed time
For **parting** us,--O, is all forgot?
All school-days' **friendship**, **childhood** innocence?
We, Hermia, like two **artificial** gods,
Have with our needles **created** both one flower,
Both on one **sampler**, **sitting** on one cushion,
Both warbling of one song, both in one key;
As if our hands, our sides, voices, and minds,
Had been **incorporate**. So we grew together,
Like to a double **cherry**, **seeming** parted;
But yet a **union** in partition,
Two lovely **berries moulded** on one stem:
So, with two seeming bodies, but one heart;
Two of the first, like coats in heraldry,
Due but to one, and crowned with one crest.
And will you **rent** our ancient love asunder,
To join with men in scorning your poor friend?
It is not **friendly**, 'tis not maidenly:

Italian

artificial: artificiale, artefatto.
bait: esca.
bare: nudo, denudare.
berries: bacche.
cannot: non potere.
cherry: ciliegia.
childhood: infanzia, fanciullezza.
counsel: consiglio, avvocato, consigliare, raccomandare, avviso.
created: creato.
false: falso, finto.
fashion: moda, modo.

foul: fallo.
friendly: amichevole, cortese, amicale, gradevole, benevole, carino, grazioso.
friendship: amicizia.
hate: odiare, odio, detestare.
hours: ore.
incorporate: incorporare, includere.
moulded: stampati.
parting: separazione, divisione.
perceive: percepire, accorgersi, scorgere, percepiamo, scorgo, scorgiamo, scorgi, scorgete,

percepite, scorgono, percepiscono.
rent: affitto, affittare, canone, noleggiare, pigione.
sampler: campionatore.
seeming: parendo, sembrando, sembrare.
sitting: sedendo, covando, seduta.
spite: dispetto.
thee: tc.
thou: tu.
ungrateful: ingrato.
union: unione, sindacato.

Our **sex**, as well as I, may **chide** you for it,
Though I alone do feel the injury.

HERMIA

I am **amazed** at your **passionate** words:
I **scorn** you not; it seems that you scorn me.

HELENA

Have you not set Lysander, as in scorn,
To follow me, and **praise** my **eyes** and face?
And made your other love, Demetrius,--
Who even but now did **spurn** me with his foot,--
To call me **goddess**, **nymph**, **divine**, and rare,
Precious, **celestial**? **Wherefore speaks** he this
To her he hates? and wherefore doth Lysander
Deny your love, so rich within his soul,
And **tender** me, forsooth, affection,
But by your **setting** on, by your consent?
What though I be not so in grace as you,
So **hung** upon with love, so fortunate;
But **miserable** most, to love unlov'd?
This you should **pity** rather than **despise**.

HERMIA

I understand not what you mean by this.

HELENA

Ay, do persever, **counterfeit sad** looks,
Make **mows** upon me when I turn my back;
Wink each at other; hold the sweet **jest** up:
This sport, well **carried**, shall be chronicled.
If you have any pity, grace, or manners,
You would not make me such an argument.
But **fare** ye well: 'tis **partly** my own fault;
Which death, or **absence**, **soon** shall **remedy**.

Italian

absence: assenza, mancanza.
amazed: sbalordito, stupito, si stupito.
carried: portato, trasportato.
celestial: celeste, celestiale.
chide: sgrida, sgrido, sgridiamo, sgridi, sgridano, sgridate, sgridare.
counterfeit: falso, falsificare.
despise: disprezzare, disprezza, disprezzano, disprezzate, disprezzi, disprezziamo, disprezzo.
divine: divino.
fare: tariffa.

goddess: dea.
hung: appeso.
jest: scherzare, scherzo.
miserable: miserabile, misero, afflitto, cattivo, triste, povero, miserevole, miserando.
mows: falcia, rasa.
nymph: ninfa.
partly: in parte, parzialmente.
passionate: appassionato, ardente.
pity: compassione, pietà.
praise: lodare, lode, elogiare, encomio,

elogio.
remedy: rimedio, medicina, rimediare.
sad: triste, afflitto.
scorn: disprezzo, disprezzare.
setting: regolazione.
sex: sesso.
soon: fra poco, presto.
speaks: parla.
spurn: rifiutare, ripulsa, rifiuto.
tender: tenero, dolce, offerta, tender.
wherefore: perchè.
ye: voi, tu.

LYSANDER
Stay, **gentle** Helena; hear my excuse;
My love, my life, my **soul**, **fair** Helena!

HELENA
O **excellent**!

HERMIA
Sweet, do not **scorn** her so.

DEMETRIUS
If she **cannot entreat**, I can **compel**.

LYSANDER
Thou canst compel no more than she entreat;
Thy **threats** have no more **strength** than her **weak** prayers.--
Helen, I love **thee**; by my life I do;
I **swear** by that which I will **lose** for thee
To **prove** him **false** that says I love thee not.

DEMETRIUS
I say I love thee more than he can do.

LYSANDER
If **thou** say so, **withdraw**, and prove it too.

DEMETRIUS
Quick, come,--

HERMIA
Lysander, whereto **tends** all this?

LYSANDER
Away, you Ethiope!

DEMETRIUS
No, no, sir:--he will
Seem to break **loose**; take on as you would follow:
But yet come not. You are a **tame** man; go!

Italian

cannot: non potere.
compel: forzare, costringere, forzate, costringete, forzo, forziamo, forzi, costringi, forza, costringono, costringo.
entreat: supplicare.
excellent: eccellente, esimio, ottimo.
fair: biondo, fiera, giusto, bazar, correttamente, bello, equo.
false: falso, finto.
gentle: mite, gentile, dolce, delicato.
loose: sciolto, lasco, slegare, slacciare, sciogliere.

lose: perdere, perdiamo, perdete, perdi, perdo, perdono.
prove: provare, proviamo, provi, provate, provano, provo, prova, comprovare, dimostrare.
scorn: disprezzo, disprezzare.
soul: anima.
strength: forza, resistenza, robustezza, potenza.
swear: giurare, giura, giuro, giuriamo, giuri, giurano, giurate, bestemmiare, imprecare.

tame: addomesticare, domestico, domare.
tends: tende.
thee: te.
thou: tu.
threats: minaccia.
weak: debole, fiacco.
withdraw: ritirare, ritiro, ritira, ritiriamo, ritiri, ritirate, ritirano, prelevare, ritirarsi, preleva, prelevano.

LYSANDER

Hang off, **thou cat**, thou **burr**: **vile** thing, let loose,
Or I will **shake thee** from me like a serpent.

HERMIA

Why are you **grown** so **rude**? what change is this,
Sweet love?

LYSANDER

Thy love! out, **tawny** Tartar, out!
Out, **loathed medicine**! **hated potion**, **hence**!

HERMIA

Do you not **jest**?

HELENA

Yes, sooth; and so do you.

LYSANDER

Demetrius, I will keep my word with thee.

DEMETRIUS

I would I had your **bond**; for I perceive
A **weak** bond holds you; I'll not **trust** your word.

LYSANDER

What! should I **hurt** her, **strike** her, **kill** her dead?
Although I hate her, I'll not **harm** her so.

HERMIA

What! can you do me **greater** harm than hate?
Hate me! **wherefore**? O me! what **news**, my love?
Am not I Hermia? Are not you Lysander?
I am as **fair** now as I was erewhile.
Since night you lov'd me; yet since night you left me:
Why then, you left me,--O, the **gods** forbid!--
In **earnest**, shall I say?

Italian

bond: legame, obbligazione, collegare, vincolo.
burr: bava.
cat: gatto, il gatto.
earnest: serio, caparra.
fair: biondo, fiera, giusto, bazar, correttamente, bello, equo.
gods: dei.
greater: maggiore.
grown: cresciuto, coltivato.
harm: danno, nuocere, danneggiare.
hate: odiare, odio, detestare.

hated: odiato.
hence: da qui, quindi.
hurt: ferire, far male, ferita, dolere.
jest: scherzare, scherzo.
kill: uccidere, ammazzare.
loathed: detestato.
medicine: medicina, medicinale, farmaco.
news: notizie, novità, notizia.
potion: pozione.
rude: scortese, rozzo, maleducato.
shake: scuotere, scuotono, scuoto,

scuotiamo, scuoti, scuotete, scossa.
strike: picchiare, colpire, battere, sciopero, scioperare, fare sciopero.
tawny: fulvo.
thee: te.
thou: tu.
trust: fiducia, trust, confidenza, affidamento.
vile: abietto.
weak: debole, fiacco.
wherefore: perchè.

LYSANDER

Ay, by my life;
And never did desire to see **thee** more.
Therefore be out of hope, of question, doubt,
Be certain, nothing truer; 'tis no jest
That I do **hate** thee and love Helena.

HERMIA

O me! you **juggler**! you cankerblossom!
You **thief** of love! What! have you come by night,
And stol'n my love's heart from him?

HELENA

Fine, i' faith!
Have you no **modesty**, no **maiden** shame,
No **touch** of **bashfulness**? What! will you tear
Impatient **answers** from my **gentle** tongue?
Fie, fie! you **counterfeit**, you **puppet**, you!

HERMIA

Puppet! why so? Ay, that way **goes** the game.
Now I **perceive** that she hath made compare
Between our statures; she hath urg'd her **height**;
And with her **personage**, her tall personage,
Her height, forsooth, she hath prevail'd with him.--
And are you **grown** so high in his esteem
Because I am so dwarfish and so low?
How low am I, **thou painted** maypole? speak;
How low am I? I am not yet so low
But that my **nails** can **reach unto thine** eyes.

HELENA

I **pray** you, though you **mock** me, gentlemen,
Let her not **hurt** me. I was never curst;
I have no **gift** at all in shrewishness;

Italian

answers: risposta, risposte.
bashfulness: timidezza.
counterfeit: falso, falsificare.
gentle: mite, gentile, dolce, delicato.
gift: regalo, dono, presente, donazione, omaggio.
goes: va.
grown: cresciuto, coltivato.
hate: odiare, odio, detestare.
height: altezza, altitudine, altura.
hurt: ferire, far male, ferita, dolere.
juggler: giocoliere.

maiden: nubile, fanciulla.
mock: deridere, deridono, derido, deridiamo, deridi, deridete, finto, beffare.
modesty: modestia, verecondia.
nails: chiodi.
painted: dipinto, verniciato.
perceive: percepire, accorgersi, scorgere, percepiamo, scorgo, scorgiamo, scorgi, scorgete, percepite, scorgono, percepiscono.
personage: personaggio.

pray: pregare, pregate, prego, preghi, prega, preghiamo, pregano.
puppet: bambola, burattino, marionetta, pupazzo.
reach: arrivare, portata, raggiungere, pervenire, estendersi.
thee: te.
thief: ladro, ladra.
thine: le tue, la tua, i tuoi, il tuo.
thou: tu.
touch: toccare, tocco, tatto.
unto: a.

I am a right **maid** for my cowardice;
Let her not **strike** me. You perhaps may think,
Because she is something **lower** than myself,
That I can **match** her.

HERMIA

Lower! **hark**, again.

HELENA

Good Hermia, do not be so **bitter** with me.
I **evermore** did love you, Hermia;
Did ever keep your counsels; never wrong'd you;
Save that, in love **unto** Demetrius,
I told him of your **stealth** unto this wood:
He **follow'd** you; for love I follow'd him;
But he hath chid me **hence**, and threaten'd me
To strike me, **spurn** me, **nay**, to **kill** me too:
And now, so you will let me **quiet** go,
To Athens will I **bear** my **folly** back,
And follow you no **farther**. Let me go:
You see how **simple** and how **fond** I am.

HERMIA

Why, get you gone: who is't that **hinders** you?

HELENA

A **foolish heart** that I leave here behind.

HERMIA

What! with Lysander?

HELENA

With Demetrius.

LYSANDER

Be not **afraid**; she shall not **harm thee**, Helena.

Italian

afraid: pauroso, inquieto, spaventato, angoscioso, impaurito.
bear: orso, produrre, ribassista, partorire, l'orso, portare.
bitter: amaro.
evermore: sempre.
farther: più lontano.
follow: seguire, seguiamo, seguite, seguo, seguono, segui.
folly: follia.
fond: tenero, affettuoso, affezionato.
foolish: sciocco, stupido, stolto,

ignorante, fesso.
hark: ascoltare.
harm: danno, nuocere, danneggiare.
heart: cuore, il cuore.
hence: da qui, quindi.
hinders: impedisce.
kill: uccidere, ammazzare.
lower: inferiore, abbassare, abbassate, abbassi, abbassiamo, abbassano, abbassa, abbasso, calare, abbattere.
maid: cameriera, ragazza.
match: fiammifero, accoppiare,

corrispondenza, partita, cerino.
nay: anzi.
quiet: calmare, tranquillo, placare, quieto, calmo, zitto, silenzioso, quiete.
simple: semplice..
spurn: rifiutare, ripulsa, rifiuto.
stealth: azione furtiva.
strike: picchiare, colpire, battere, sciopero, scioperare, fare sciopero.
thee: te.
unto: a.

DEMETRIUS
No, **sir**, she shall not, **though** you take her part.

HELENA
O, when she's **angry**, she is **keen** and shrewd:
She was a **vixen** when she went to school;
And, though she be but little, she is **fierce**.

HERMIA
Little again! nothing but **low** and little!--
Why will you **suffer** her to **flout** me thus?
Let me come to her.

LYSANDER
                    Get you **gone**, you dwarf;
You minimus, of hind'ring knot-grass made;
You **bead**, you **acorn**.

DEMETRIUS
                    You are too officious
In her behalf that scorns your services.
Let her **alone**: **speak** not of Helena;
Take not her part; for if thou dost intend
Never so little show of love to her,
Thou shalt aby it.

LYSANDER
                    Now she holds me not;
Now **follow**, if thou dar'st, to try **whose** right,
Of **thine** or **mine**, is most in Helena.

DEMETRIUS
Follow! **nay**, I'll go with **thee**, **cheek** by jole.

[Exeunt LYSANDER and DEMETRIUS.]

Italian

acorn: ghianda.
alone: solo, da solo, solamente.
angry: arrabbiato, irato, stizzito.
bead: perlina.
cheek: guancia, la guancia.
fierce: feroce.
flout: schernire.
follow: seguire, seguiamo, seguite,
  seguo, seguono, segui.
gone: andato.
keen: aguzzo, acuto, tagliente, affilato.
low: basso.

mine: miniera, mina, minare, estrarre.
nay: anzi.
sir: signore.
speak: parlare, parla, parlo, parliamo,
  parli, parlate, parlano, favellare.
suffer: soffrire, soffri, soffro, soffrono,
  soffrite, soffriamo, patire, subire,
  patiamo, patite, patiscono.
thee: te.
thine: le tue, la tua, i tuoi, il tuo.
thou: tu.
vixen: megera.

whose: di chi, il cui.

HERMIA

You, **mistress**, all this **coil** is 'long of you:
Nay, go not back.

HELENA

I will not **trust** you, I;
Nor **longer** stay in your curst company.
Your hands than **mine** are quicker for a fray;
My **legs** are longer **though**, to run away.
[Exit.]

HERMIA

I am amaz'd, and know not what to say.
[Exit, **pursuing** HELENA.]

OBERON

This is **thy negligence**: still thou mistak'st,
Or else commit'st thy knaveries willfully.

PUCK

Believe me, king of shadows, I mistook.
Did not you tell me I should know the man
By the Athenian **garments** he had on?
And so far **blameless proves** my enterprise
That I have 'nointed an Athenian's eyes:
And so far am I **glad** it so did sort,
As this their jangling I **esteem** a **sport**.

OBERON

Thou seest these lovers **seek** a place to fight;
Hie therefore, Robin, **overcast** the night;
The **starry** welkin **cover** thou anon
With drooping **fog**, as black as Acheron,
And lead these **testy** rivals so astray
As one come not within another's way.
Like to Lysander sometime **frame** thy tongue,

Italian

blameless: irreprensibile.
coil: bobina, rotolo.
cover: coprire, coperta, copertura, copertina, percorrere, coperchio, legatura.
esteem: stima, rispetto, stimare, considerazione, considerare, rispettare, riguardo.
fog: nebbia, annebbiare.
frame: telaio, intelaiatura, cornice, fotogramma, incorniciare, struttura, inquadrare, immagine, incastellatura,

ordinata.
garments: indumenti.
glad: contento, felice, lieto.
legs: gambe.
longer: oltre, più lungo.
mine: miniera, mina, minare, estrarre.
mistress: padrona.
negligence: negligenza, trascuratezza, condotta negligente.
overcast: coperto.
proves: prova.
pursuing: perseguendo.

seek: cercare, cercano, cerchiamo, cercate, cerchi, cerco, cerca.
sport: sport.
starry: stellato.
testy: stizzoso, irritabile.
thou: tu.
thy: tuo.
trust: fiducia, trust, confidenza, affidamento.

Then stir Demetrius up with bitter wrong;
And sometime **rail thou** like Demetrius;
And from each other look thou lead them thus,
Till o'er their brows death-counterfeiting sleep
With **leaden** legs and **batty** wings doth creep:
Then **crush** this **herb** into Lysander's eye;
Whose **liquor** hath this **virtuous** property,
To take from **thence** all **error** with his might
And make his eyeballs **roll** with **wonted** sight.
When they next **wake**, all this derision
Shall seem a dream and **fruitless** vision;
And back to Athens shall the lovers wend
With league whose date till death shall never end.
Whiles I in this **affair** do **thee** employ,
I'll to my queen, and **beg** her Indian boy;
And then I will her **charmed** eye release
From monster's view, and all things shall be peace.

PUCK
My fairy lord, this must be done with haste,
For night's **swift dragons** cut the clouds full fast;
And **yonder** shines Aurora's harbinger,
At whose approach ghosts, **wandering** here and there,
Troop home to churchyards: **damned** spirits all,
That in cross-ways and floods have burial,
Already to their **wormy** beds are gone;
For fear **lest** day should look their shames upon
They wilfully **exile** themselves from light,
And must for **aye consort** with black-brow'd night.

OBERON
But we are spirits of another sort:
I with the morning's love have **oft** made sport;

Italian

affair: affare, faccenda, caso.
aye: sì.
batty: pazzo.
beg: mendicare, mendicano, mendica, mendicate, mendico, mendichiamo, mendichi, chiedere, elemosinare, supplicare.
charmed: affascinato.
consort: consorte, coniuge.
crush: schiacciare, schiacciamento, accasciare, frantumare.
damned: dannato, maledetto.

dragons: draghi.
error: errore, sbaglio, fallo.
exile: esiliare, esilio, esule, bandire, esiliato.
fruitless: infruttuoso, inutile.
herb: erba, erbe.
leaden: di piombo.
lest: affinchè non, per paura che.
liquor: liquore.
oft: spesso.
rail: rotaia, parapetto, guida.
roll: rullo, panino, rotolare, rotolo,

rullio, rollio, cilindrare.
swift: rondone, veloce, rapido, celere.
thee: te.
thence: di là.
thou: tu.
virtuous: virtuoso.
wake: svegliare, scia, destare.
wandering: vagando, peregrinazione.
wonted: usuale, consueto, solito.
wormy: bacato.
yonder: là, laggiù.

A Midsummer Night's Dream

And, like a **forester**, the groves may tread
Even **till** the **eastern gate**, all fiery-red,
Opening on Neptune with **fair blessed** beams,
Turns into **yellow gold** his salt-green streams.
But, **notwithstanding**, **haste**; make no delay:
We may effect this business yet ere day.

[**Exit** OBERON.]

PUCK

    Up and down, up and down;
    I will lead them up and down:
    I am fear'd in **field** and town.
    Goblin, lead them up and down.
Here comes one.

[**Enter** LYSANDER.]

LYSANDER

Where art **thou**, **proud** Demetrius? speak thou now.

PUCK

Here, **villain**; **drawn** and **ready**. Where art thou?

LYSANDER

I will be with **thee straight**.

PUCK

                      Follow me, then,
To plainer ground.

[Exit LYSANDER as following the voice.]

[Enter DEMETRIUS.]

DEMETRIUS

            Lysander! speak again.
Thou **runaway**, thou **coward**, art thou fled?
Speak. In some **bush**? where dost thou **hide thy** head?

Italian

blessed: benedetto, beato.
bush: arbusto, cespuglio, boccola, bussola.
coward: codardo, vigliacco.
drawn: disegnato.
eastern: orientale.
enter: entrare, entra, entrano, entrate, entri, entriamo, entro, invio.
exit: uscita, uscire, l'uscita.
fair: biondo, fiera, giusto, bazar, correttamente, bello, equo.
field: campo, settore.

forester: guardia forestale, guardaboschi.
gate: cancello, porta, saracinesca, paratoia, uscita.
gold: oro, d'oro.
haste: fretta, furia.
hide: nascondere, nascondo, nascondiamo, nascondono, nascondete, nascondi, pelle, nascondersi, pellame, celare, occultare.
notwithstanding: nonostante.

proud: orgoglioso, fiero.
ready: pronto, disposto.
runaway: fuggiasco.
straight: diritto, destro, dritto, direttamente.
thee: te.
thou: tu.
thy: tuo.
till: finchè, coltivare, cassa, fino, arare.
villain: furfante.
yellow: giallo.

PUCK

    Thou **coward**, **art thou** bragging to the stars,

    Telling the bushes that thou look'st for wars,

    And **wilt** not come? Come, **recreant**; come, thou child;

    I'll **whip thee** with a **rod**: he is defiled

    That **draws** a **sword** on thee.

DEMETRIUS

                      Yea, art thou there?

PUCK

    Follow my voice; we'll try no **manhood** here.

    [Exeunt.]

    [Re-enter LYSANDER.]

LYSANDER

    He **goes** before me, and still **dares** me on;

    When I come where he **calls**, then he is gone.

    The **villain** is much **lighter** heeled than I:

    I follow'd **fast**, but faster he did fly;

    That **fallen** am I in **dark uneven** way,

    And here will **rest** me. Come, thou **gentle** day!

    [Lies down.]

    For if but once thou show me **thy grey** light,

    I'll find Demetrius, and **revenge** this spite.

    [Sleeps.]

    [Re-enter PUCK and DEMETRIUS.]

PUCK

    Ho, ho, ho, ho! Coward, why com'st thou not?

DEMETRIUS

    Abide me, if thou dar'st; for well I wot

    Thou runn'st before me, **shifting** every place;

Italian

art: arte, l'arte.
calls: chiama.
coward: codardo, vigliacco.
dares: osa.
dark: scuro, oscuro, buio, oscurità, tenebroso.
draws: disegna.
fallen: caduto.
fast: veloce, digiuno, velocemente, presto, digiunare, rapido.
gentle: mite, gentile, dolce, delicato.
goes: va.

grey: grigio, bigio.
lighter: accendino, chiatta, bettolina.
manhood: virilità.
recreant: codardo.
rest: riposo, riposarsi, riposare, resto, pausa.
revenge: vendetta.
rod: barra, verga, bacchetta, asta.
shifting: spostare, spostamento.
sword: spada.
thee: te.
thou: tu.

thy: tuo.
uneven: irregolare, ineguale.
villain: furfante.
whip: frusta, frustare, sferza, sbattere.
wilt: appassire, appassisco, appassiscono, appassisci, appassiamo, appassite.

And dar'st not **stand**, **nor** look me in the face.
Where **art thou**?

PUCK

           Come **hither**; I am here.

DEMETRIUS

Nay, then, thou mock'st me.
Thou shalt **buy** this dear,
If ever I **thy** face by **daylight** see:
Now, go thy way. **Faintness** constraineth me
To **measure** out my **length** on this **cold** bed.--
By day's **approach** look to be visited.
[Lies down and **sleeps**.]

[**Enter** HELENA.]

HELENA

O **weary** night, O long and **tedious** night,
Abate thy **hours**! **Shine** comforts from the east,
That I may back to Athens by daylight,
From these that my **poor** company detest:--
And sleep, that sometimes shuts up sorrow's eye,
Steal me awhile from **mine** own company.
[Sleeps.]

PUCK

Yet but three? Come one more;
Two of both kinds **makes** up four.
Here she **comes**, curst and sad:--
Cupid is a **knavish** lad,
Thus to make poor females **mad**.

[Enter HERMIA.]

HERMIA

Never so weary, never so in woe,

Italian

approach: accesso, approccio, avvicinare, avvicinamento, avvicinarsi, accostare.
art: arte, l'arte.
buy: comprare, comperare, acquisto, acquistare, compra.
cold: freddo, raffreddore.
comes: viene.
daylight: luce del giorno.
enter: entrare, entra, entrano, entrate, entri, entriamo, entro, invio.
faintness: debolezza.

hither: qui, quà.
hours: ore.
knavish: furfantesco, da briccone, disonesto.
length: lunghezza, durata.
mad: matto, pazzo, arrabbiato, rabbioso, folle.
makes: fa, commette.
measure: misura, misurare, provvedimento.
mine: miniera, mina, minare, estrarre.
nor: ne.

poor: povero, cattivo.
shine: risplendere, brillare, lustro, splendere.
sleep: sonno, dormire, dormi, dormiamo, dormite, dormo, dormono.
stand: stare in piedi, granaio, alzarsi, bancarella.
tedious: noioso, tedioso.
thou: tu.
thy: tuo.
weary: stanco, stancare, fiacco.

Bedabbled with the **dew**, and **torn** with briers;
I can no further **crawl**, no further go;
My **legs** can keep no **pace** with my desires.
Here will I **rest** me **till** the **break** of day.
Heavens **shield** Lysander, if they mean a fray!
[Lies down.]

PUCK

On the ground
Sleep sound:
I'll apply
To your eye,
Gentle **lover**, remedy.
[Squeezing the **juice** on LYSANDER'S eye.]
When **thou** wak'st,
Thou tak'st
True delight
In the sight
Of **thy former** lady's eye:
And the country **proverb** known,
That every man should take his own,
In your **waking** shall be shown:
Jack shall have Jill;
Nought shall go ill;
The man shall have his **mare** again, and all shall be well.
[**Exit** PUCK.--DEMETRIUS, HELENA &c, sleep.]

Italian

break: rompere, rottura, spezzare, rompersi, frattura, pausa, schiantare, infrangere, sosta, spaccare.
crawl: strisciare.
dew: rugiada.
exit: uscita, uscire, l'uscita.
former: precedente, passato.
juice: succo, sugo.
legs: gambe.
lover: amante.
mare: cavalla.
pace: passo, andatura, velocità.

proverb: proverbio.
rest: riposo, riposarsi, riposare, resto, pausa.
shield: scudo, riparo, proteggere, schermo, schermare.
thou: tu.
thy: tuo.
till: finchè, coltivare, cassa, fino, arare.
torn: strappato, lacero.
waking: svegliare.

ACT IV

SCENE I. THE WOOD.

[Enter TITANIA and BOTTOM; PEASBLOSSOM, COBWEB, MOTH, MUSTARDSEED, and other FAIRIES **attending**; OBERON behind, unseen.]

TITANIA
> Come, **sit thee** down upon this **flowery** bed,
> While I **thy amiable** cheeks do coy,
> And **stick** musk-roses in thy **sleek smooth** head,
> And **kiss** thy **fair** large **ears**, my **gentle joy**.

BOTTOM
> Where's Peasblossom?

PEASBLOSSOM
> Ready.

BOTTOM
> Scratch my head, Peasblossom.--
> Where's Monsieur Cobweb?

COBWEB
> Ready.

Italian

amiable: amabile.
attending: visitando, curando, assistendo.
ears: orecchie.
fair: biondo, fiera, giusto, bazar, correttamente, bello, equo.
flowery: fiorito.
gentle: mite, gentile, dolce, delicato.
joy: gioia.
kiss: bacio, baciare, baciarsi.
sit: sedere, sediamo, siedono, siedi, sedete, siedo, covare, covo, covi,
cova, covate.
sleek: lisciare, lucido.
smooth: liscio, piano, levigare, spianare, lisciare.
stick: bastone, appiccicare, bastoncino, attaccare, incollare, ficcare, bacchetta.
thee: te.
thy: tuo.

BOTTOM

Monsieur Cobweb; good monsieur, get you your **weapons** in your hand and kill me a red-hipped humble-bee on the **top** of a **thistle**; and, good monsieur, bring me the honey-bag. Do not **fret yourself** too much in the action, monsieur; and, good monsieur, have a care the honey-bag break not; I would be **loath** to have you overflown with a honey-bag, signior.-- Where's Monsieur Mustardseed?

MUSTARDSEED

Ready.

BOTTOM

Give me your neif, Monsieur Mustardseed.
Pray you, leave your **curtsy**, good monsieur.

MUSTARDSEED

What's your will?

BOTTOM

Nothing, good monsieur, but to help Cavalero Cobweb to **scratch**. I must to the barber's, monsieur; for methinks I am marvellous **hairy** about the face; and I am such a tender ass, if my hair do but **tickle** me I must scratch.

TITANIA

What, **wilt** thou hear some **music**, my sweet love?

BOTTOM

I have a **reasonable** good ear in music; let us have the **tongs** and the **bones**.

TITANIA

Or say, sweet love, what thou desirest to eat.

BOTTOM

Truly, a **peck** of provender; I could **munch** your good **dry oats**. Methinks I have a great desire to a **bottle** of **hay**: good hay, sweet hay, hath no **fellow**.

TITANIA

I have a venturous fairy that shall seek
The squirrel's **hoard**, and fetch thee new **nuts**.

Italian

bones: ossa.
bottle: bottiglia, imbottigliare, la bottiglia.
curtsy: inchino, riverenza.
dry: secco, seccare, asciutto, essiccare, asciugare.
fellow: uomo.
fret: agitazione, consumare, greca.
hair: capelli, capello, pelo, capigliatura.
hairy: peloso, capelluto, villoso, irsuto.
hay: fieno.

hoard: ammasso, ammassare.
loath: contrario, restio.
munch: sgranocchia, sgranocchio, sgranocchiate, sgranocchiamo, sgranocchi, sgranocchiano, masticare rumorosamente, sgranocchiare.
music: musica, la musica.
nuts: matto.
oats: avena.
peck: beccare.
reasonable: ragionevole, sensato.
scratch: graffiare, graffio, grattare,

raschiare, graffiatura, scalfire, unghiata.
thistle: cardo.
tickle: stimolare, stuzzicare, solleticare, solletico.
tongs: pinzette.
top: cima.
weapons: armi.
wilt: appassire, appassisco, appassiscono, appassisci, appassiamo, appassite.
yourself: ti.

BOTTOM

I had rather have a **handful** or two of **dried** peas. But, I pray you, let none of your people stir me; I have an **exposition** of sleep come upon me.

TITANIA

Sleep thou, and I will wind thee in my arms.
Fairies, be gone, and be all **ways** away.
So doth the **woodbine** the sweet honeysuckle
Gently entwist,--the **female ivy** so
Enrings the barky fingers of the elm.
O, how I love thee! how I **dote** on thee!

[They sleep.]

[OBERON **advances**. Enter PUCK.]

OBERON

Welcome, good Robin. Seest thou this sweet sight?
Her **dotage** now I do begin to pity.
For, **meeting** her of **late** behind the wood,
Seeking sweet favours for this **hateful** fool,
I did **upbraid** her and **fall** out with her:
For she his hairy temples then had rounded
With **coronet** of fresh and **fragrant** flowers;
And that same dew, which sometime on the buds
Was **wont** to **swell** like round and **orient** pearls,
Stood now within the pretty flow'rets' eyes,
Like tears that did their own **disgrace** bewail.
When I had, at my **pleasure**, **taunted** her,
And she, in mild **terms**, begg'd my patience,
I then did ask of her her changeling child;
Which straight she gave me, and her fairy sent
To bear him to my bower in fairy-land.
And now I have the boy, I will undo
This hateful **imperfection** of her eyes.

Italian

advances: avanzamenti.
coronet: corona nobiliare, corona.
disgrace: vergogna, disgrazia, disonorare, disonore.
dotage: rimbambimento.
dote: essere rimbambito.
dried: secco.
exposition: esposizione.
fall: cadere, caduta, autunno, cadono, cado, cadiamo, cadi, cadete, diminuire, calo, piombare.
female: femmina, femminile.

fragrant: profumato, fragrante, odoroso.
handful: manciata.
hateful: odioso.
imperfection: imperfezione.
ivy: edera.
late: tardi, tardo, in ritardo, tardivo.
meeting: incontrando, convegno, riunione, incontro, adunanza, comizio, assemblea.
orient: oriente, orientare.
pleasure: piacere, gradimento.

swell: gonfiare, dilatare, rigonfiamento, mare lungo, crescendo.
taunted: schernito, rinfacciato.
terms: condizioni.
upbraid: rimproverare, rimprovera, rimproverano, rimproverate, rimproveri, rimproveriamo, rimprovero.
ways: modi.
wont: avvezzo, abitudine.
woodbine: caprifoglio.

And, **gentle** Puck, take this **transformed** scalp
From off the head of this Athenian swain,
That he awaking when the other do,
May all to Athens back again repair,
And think no more of this night's accidents
But as the **fierce vexation** of a dream.
But first I will **release** the **fairy** queen.
  Be as **thou** wast **wont** to be;
[Touching her eyes with an herb.]
  See as thou was wont to see.
  Dian's **bud** o'er Cupid's flower
  Hath such **force** and **blessed** power.
Now, my Titania; **wake** you, my **sweet** queen.

TITANIA
My Oberon! what visions have I seen!
Methought I was enamour'd of an **ass**.

OBERON
There lies your love.

TITANIA
     How came these things to pass?
O, how **mine** eyes do **loathe** his **visage** now!

OBERON
Silence awhile.--Robin, take off this head.
Titania, **music call**; and **strike** more dead
Than **common sleep**, of all these five, the sense.

TITANIA
Music, ho! music; such as charmeth sleep.

PUCK
Now when thou wak'st, with **thine** own fool's eyes **peep**.

Italian

ass: asino, ciuco, somaro, culo.
blessed: benedetto, beato.
bud: bocciolo, germoglio, germogliare, gemma.
call: chiamare, chiami, chiamiamo, chiamo, chiamano, chiama, chiamate, chiamata, appello.
common: comune, volgare, ordinario.
fairy: fata.
fierce: feroce.
force: forza, forzare, costringere, vigore.

gentle: mite, gentile, dolce, delicato.
loathe: detestare, detesti, detesto, detestiamo, detestano, detesta, detestate, avere in orrore.
mine: miniera, mina, minare, estrarre.
music: musica, la musica.
peep: occhieggiare, pigolio, pigolare, sbirciare.
release: liberare, rilasciare, rilascio, disinnesto, liberazione, svincolo, versione.
sleep: sonno, dormire, dormi,

dormiamo, dormite, dormo, dormono.
strike: picchiare, colpire, battere, sciopero, scioperare, fare sciopero.
sweet: dolce, soave, caramella.
thine: le tue, la tua, i tuoi, il tuo.
thou: tu.
transformed: trasformato.
vexation: irritazione.
visage: viso, volto.
wake: svegliare, scia, destare.
wont: avvezzo, abitudine.

OBERON

Sound, **music**. [Still music.] Come, my **queen**, take hands with me,
And **rock** the **ground** whereon these sleepers be.
Now **thou** and I are new in amity,
And will to-morrow **midnight** solemnly
Dance in Duke Theseus' house triumphantly,
And **bless** it to all **fair** prosperity:
There shall the **pairs** of **faithful** lovers be
Wedded, with Theseus, all in jollity.

PUCK

Fairy **king**, **attend** and mark;
I do **hear** the morning **lark**.

OBERON

Then, my queen, in **silence** sad,
Trip we after night's shade.
We the **globe** can **compass** soon,
Swifter than the wand'ring **moon**.

TITANIA

Come, my **lord**; and in our flight,
Tell me how it came this night
That I **sleeping** here was found
With these mortals on the ground.

[Exeunt. Horns **sound** within.]

[Enter THESEUS, HIPPOLYTA, EGEUS, and Train.]

THESEUS

Go, one of you, find out the forester;--
For now our **observation** is perform'd;
And since we have the vaward of the day,
My love shall hear the music of my hounds,--
Uncouple in the **western valley**; go:--

Italian

attend: visitare, curare, assistere, curiamo, curi, curo, curano, visitate, visitiamo, cura, visiti.
bless: benedire, benedi', benedite, benedicono, benedico, benedici, benediciamo.
compass: bussola, la bussola, compasso.
fair: biondo, fiera, giusto, bazar, correttamente, bello, equo.
faithful: fedele, leale.
globe: globo, mappamondo, sfera.

ground: suolo, fondo, terra, massa, terreno.
hear: udire, odono, odi, odo, udite, udiamo, sentire, sentono, sento, sentite, senti.
king: re.
lark: allodola.
lord: signore.
midnight: mezzanotte.
moon: luna, la luna.
music: musica, la musica.
observation: osservazione.

pairs: pari.
queen: regina.
rock: roccia, masso, cullare, dondolare, ondeggiare.
silence: silenzio.
sleeping: dormendo, addormentato.
sound: suono, sonare, suonare, solido, sondare, sano, scandagliare, rumore, sonda.
thou: tu.
valley: valle, vallata.
western: occidentale.

Despatch, I say, and find the forester.--
[Exit an ATTENDANT.]
We will, **fair queen**, up to the mountain's top,
And **mark** the **musical** confusion
Of hounds and **echo** in conjunction.

HIPPOLYTA

I was with Hercules and Cadmus once
When in a **wood** of Crete they bay'd the bear
With hounds of Sparta: never did I hear
Such **gallant chiding**; for, **besides** the groves,
The skies, the fountains, every **region** near
Seem'd all one **mutual cry**: I never heard
So musical a **discord**, such **sweet thunder**.

THESEUS

My hounds are bred out of the Spartan kind,
So flew'd, so sanded; and their heads are hung
With **ears** that **sweep** away the morning dew;
Crook-knee'd and dew-lap'd like Thessalian bulls;
Slow in **pursuit**, but match'd in **mouth** like bells,
Each under each. A cry more tuneable
Was never holla'd to, **nor** cheer'd with horn,
In Crete, in Sparta, nor in Thessaly.
Judge when you hear.--But, **soft**, what **nymphs** are these?

EGEUS

My lord, this is my **daughter** here asleep;
And this Lysander; this Demetrius is;
This Helena, old Nedar's Helena:
I **wonder** of their being here together.

THESEUS

No **doubt** they **rose** up early to observe
The **rite** of May; and, **hearing** our intent,

Italian

besides: inoltre, d'altronde.
chiding: sgridando.
cry: piangere, grido, gridare, urlare.
daughter: figlia, figliola, figliuola, la figlia.
discord: disaccordo.
doubt: dubitare, dubbio.
ears: orecchie.
echo: eco, echeggiare.
fair: biondo, fiera, giusto, bazar, correttamente, bello, equo.
gallant: galante, coraggioso, valoroso.

hearing: udendo, sentendo, udito, udienza, ascolto.
mark: segno, marcare, marco, marchio, contrassegnare, marca, segnare, contrassegno, voto.
mouth: bocca, imboccatura, foce, la bocca, apertura.
musical: musicale, musical.
mutual: reciproco.
nor: ne.
nymphs: ninfa.
pursuit: inseguimento, ricerca.

queen: regina.
region: regione, zona.
rite: rito.
rose: rosa.
soft: dolce, molle, soffice, morbido, tenero.
sweep: spazzare, scopare, spazzata.
sweet: dolce, soave, caramella.
thunder: tuono, tuonare.
wonder: stupirsi, stupore, meraviglia, domandarsi, meravigliarsi.
wood: legno, bosco, selva, legna.

Came here in **grace** of our solemnity.--
But **speak**, Egeus; is not this the day
That Hermia should give answer of her **choice**?

EGEUS

It is, my lord.

THESEUS

Go, **bid** the huntsmen **wake** them with their horns.
[Horns, and **shout** within. DEMETRIUS, LYSANDER,HERMIA, and
HELENA **awake** and start up.]
Good-morrow, friends. **Saint** Valentine is past;
Begin these wood-birds but to **couple** now?

LYSANDER

Pardon, my lord.
[He and the rest **kneel** to THESEUS.]

THESEUS

　　　　　　　　　　　　I **pray** you all, **stand** up.
I know you two are **rival** enemies;
How comes this **gentle concord** in the world,
That **hatred** is so far from jealousy
To **sleep** by hate, and **fear** no **enmity**?

LYSANDER

My lord, I shall **reply** amazedly,
Half 'sleep, half **waking**; but as yet, I swear,
I **cannot truly** say how I came here:
But, as I think,--for truly would I speak--
And now I do bethink me, so it is,--
I came with Hermia **hither**: our intent
Was to be gone from Athens, where we might be,
Without the **peril** of the Athenian law.

Italian

awake: sveglio, svegliarsi.
bid: offerta, offrire, chiedere.
cannot: non potere.
choice: scelta.
concord: accordo.
couple: coppia, accoppiare, paio, consorti, coniugi, agganciare.
enmity: inimicizia.
fear: paura, temere, angoscia, timore, aver timore.
gentle: mite, gentile, dolce, delicato.
grace: grazia.

hate: odiare, odio, detestare.
hatred: odio.
hither: qui, quà.
kneel: inginocchiarsi.
peril: pericolo.
pray: pregare, pregate, prego, preghi, prega, preghiamo, pregano.
reply: risposta, rispondere, replicare, replica.
rival: rivale.
saint: santo.
shout: gridare, grido, urlo, sbraitare,

urlare.
sleep: sonno, dormire, dormi, dormiamo, dormite, dormo, dormono.
speak: parlare, parla, parlo, parliamo, parli, parlate, parlano, favellare.
stand: stare in piedi, granaio, alzarsi, bancarella.
truly: davvero, infatti, veramente.
wake: svegliare, scia, destare.
waking: svegliare.

EGEUS

Enough, enough, my lord; you have enough;
I **beg** the law, the law upon his head.--
They would have stol'n away, they would, Demetrius,
Thereby to have **defeated** you and me:
You of your **wife**, and me of my **consent**,--
Of my consent that she should be your wife.

DEMETRIUS

My lord, fair Helen told me of their stealth,
Of this their **purpose hither** to this wood;
And I in **fury** hither follow'd them,
Fair Helena in **fancy** following me.
But, my good lord, I wot not by what power,--
But by some power it is,--my love to Hermia,
Melted as the snow--seems to me now
As the **remembrance** of an **idle** gawd
Which in my **childhood** I did **dote** upon:
And all the faith, the **virtue** of my heart,
The **object** and the **pleasure** of mine eye,
Is only Helena. To her, my lord,
Was I betroth'd ere I saw Hermia:
But, like a **sickness**, did I **loathe** this food;
But, as in health, come to my **natural** taste,
Now I do wish it, love it, long for it,
And will for **evermore** be true to it.

THESEUS

Fair lovers, you are **fortunately** met:
Of this **discourse** we more will hear anon.--
Egeus, I will overbear your will;
For in the **temple**, by and by with us,
These **couples** shall **eternally** be knit.

Italian

beg: mendicare, mendicano, mendica, mendicate, mendico, mendichiamo, mendichi, chiedere, elemosinare, supplicare.
childhood: infanzia, fanciullezza.
consent: consenso, concordare, essere d'accordo, accordo, benestare, assenso, acconsentire.
couples: coppia.
defeated: sconfitto, sconfitta, sconfiggere.
discourse: discorso.

dote: essere rimbambito.
eternally: eternamente.
evermore: sempre.
fancy: figurarsi, capriccio, immaginazione.
fortunately: fortunatamente, per fortuna.
fury: furia, furore.
hither: qui, quà.
idle: ozioso, pigro, folle, inattivo.
loathe: detestare, detesti, detesto, detestiamo, detestano, detesta,

detestate, avere in orrore.
natural: naturale.
object: oggetto, cosa, scopo.
pleasure: piacere, gradimento.
purpose: scopo, proposito, fine, intenzione.
remembrance: rimembranza, ricordo, memoria.
sickness: malattia.
temple: tempia, tempio.
virtue: virtù.
wife: moglie, la moglie.

And, for the morning now is something worn,
Our purpos'd **hunting** shall be set aside.--
Away with us to Athens, three and three,
We'll **hold** a **feast** in great solemnity.--
Come, Hippolyta.
[Exeunt THESEUS, HIPPOLYTA, EGEUS, and Train.]

DEMETRIUS

These things **seem** small and undistinguishable,
Like far-off **mountains turned** into clouds.

HERMIA

Methinks I see these things with parted eye,
When every thing seems **double**.

HELENA

So methinks:
And I have found Demetrius like a jewel.
Mine own, and not **mine** own.

DEMETRIUS

It seems to me
That yet we **sleep**, we dream.--Do not you think
The **duke** was here, and **bid** us **follow** him?

HERMIA

Yea, and my father.

HELENA

And Hippolyta.

LYSANDER

And he did bid us follow to the **temple**.

DEMETRIUS

Why, then, we are **awake**: let's follow him;
And by the way let us **recount** our dreams.

[Exeunt.]

Italian

awake: sveglio, svegliarsi.
bid: offerta, offrire, chiedere.
double: doppio, sosia, raddoppiare,
 duplice.
duke: duca.
feast: banchetto, festa.
follow: seguire, seguiamo, seguite,
 seguo, seguono, segui.
hold: tenere, stiva, stretta, mantenere,
 ritenere.
hunting: cacciando, caccia.
mine: miniera, mina, minare, estrarre.

mountains: montagne.
recount: narrare, raccontare.
seem: parere, paiono, paiamo, pari,
 paio, parete, sembrare, sembra,
 sembrano, sembrate, sembri.
sleep: sonno, dormire, dormi,
 dormiamo, dormite, dormo,
 dormono.
temple: tempia, tempio.
turned: girato, svoltato, cambiato.

[As they go out, BOTTOM awakes.]

BOTTOM

When my **cue** comes, call me, and I will answer. My next is 'Most fair Pyramus.'--Heigh-ho!--Peter Quince! **Flute**, the bellows-mender! **Snout**, the tinker! Starveling! God's my life, stol'n **hence**, and left me **asleep**! I have had a most **rare vision**. I have had a **dream**--past the **wit** of man to say what dream it was.--Man is but an **ass** if he go about to **expound** this dream. Methought I was--there is no man can tell what. Methought I was, and methought I had,--but man is but a **patched fool**, if he will **offer** to say what methought I had. The eye of man hath not **heard**, the ear of man hath not seen; man's hand is not able to **taste**, his **tongue** to **conceive**, nor his heart to report, what my dream was. I will get Peter Quince to write a **ballad** of this dream: it shall be called Bottom's Dream, because it hath no **bottom**; and I will **sing** it in the **latter** end of a play, before the **duke**: peradventure, to make it the more **gracious**, I shall sing it at her death.

[Exit.]

SCENE II. **ATHENS**. A ROOM IN QUINCE'S HOUSE.

[Enter QUINCE, FLUTE, SNOUT, and STARVELING.]

QUINCE

Have you **sent** to Bottom's house? is he come home yet?

STARVELING

He **cannot** be heard of. Out of doubt, he is **transported**.

FLUTE

If he come not, then the play is **marred**; it goes not
forward, doth it?

Italian

asleep: addormentato.
ass: asino, ciuco, somaro, culo.
athens: Atene.
ballad: ballata.
bottom: fondo, basso, carena.
cannot: non potere.
conceive: concepire, concepiamo, concepisci, concepisco, concepiscono, concepite.
cue: stecca.
dream: sogno, sognare.
duke: duca.

ear: orecchio, spiga, l'orecchio, pannocchia.
expound: spiegare.
flute: flauto, scanalatura.
fool: babbeo, sciocco, allocco, ingannare.
gracious: grazioso.
hence: da qui, quindi.
latter: ultimo.
marred: guastato, rovinato, sciupato.
offer: offerta, offrire, proporre, presentare, proposta.

patched: rappezzato.
rare: raro, al sangue.
sent: mandato, spedito.
sing: cantare, canta, cantano, cantate, canti, cantiamo, canto.
snout: muso, sigaretta, grifo, grugno.
taste: gustare, gusto, assaggiare, sapore.
tongue: lingua, linguetta, la lingua.
transported: trasportato.
vision: visione, vista.
wit: arguzia.

QUINCE

It is not possible: you have not a man in all Athens able to **discharge** Pyramus but he.

FLUTE

No; he hath **simply** the best **wit** of any **handicraft** man in Athens.

QUINCE

Yea, and the best person too: and he is a very **paramour** for a **sweet** voice.

FLUTE

You must say **paragon**: a paramour is, God **bless** us, a thing of **naught**.

[**Enter** SNUG.]

SNUG

Masters, the **duke** is **coming** from the **temple**; and there is two or three lords and **ladies** more **married**: if our **sport** had gone **forward**, we had all been made men.

FLUTE

O sweet **bully** Bottom! Thus hath he **lost** sixpence a day during his life; he could not have 'scaped sixpence a-day; an the duke had not given him sixpence a-day for **playing** Pyramus, I'll be hanged; he would have **deserved** it: sixpence a-day in Pyramus, or nothing.

[Enter BOTTOM.]

BOTTOM

Where are these lads? where are these **hearts**?

QUINCE

Bottom!--O most **courageous** day! O most **happy hour**!

BOTTOM

Masters, I am to **discourse** wonders: but ask me not what; for if I tell you, I am not true Athenian. I will tell you **everything**, right as it **fell** out.

QUINCE

Let us hear, sweet Bottom.

Italian

bless: benedire, benedi', benedite, benedicono, benedico, benedici, benediciamo.
bully: prepotente.
coming: venendo.
courageous: coraggioso.
deserved: meritato.
discharge: scarico, scarica, portata, scaricare.
discourse: discorso.
duke: duca.
enter: entrare, entra, entrano, entrate, entri, entriamo, entro, invio.
everything: tutto.
fell: abbattere.
forward: avanti, spedire, attaccante, in avanti, inoltrare.
handicraft: artigianato, mestiere.
happy: felice, contento, lieto, beato.
hear: udire, odono, odi, odo, udite, udiamo, sentire, sentono, sento, sentite, senti.
hearts: cuori.
hour: ora, l'ora.
ladies: signore.
lost: perso, perduto, smarrito.
married: sposato, si sposato.
naught: nulla, zero.
paragon: esemplare.
paramour: amante, drudo.
playing: giocando, suonando.
simply: semplicemente.
sport: sport.
sweet: dolce, soave, caramella.
temple: tempia, tempio.
wit: arguzia.

BOTTOM

Not   a **word** of me. All that I will tell you is, that the **duke** hath **dined**. Get your **apparel** together; good strings to your **beards**, new ribbons to your **pumps**; meet **presently** at the **palace**; every man look over his part; for the **short** and the long is, our play is **preferred**. In any case, let Thisby have **clean linen**; and let not him that **plays** the **lion** pare his **nails**, for they shall **hang** out for the lion's claws. And, most **dear actors**, **eat** no onions **nor** garlick, for we are to **utter sweet breath**; and I do not **doubt** but to **hear** them say it is a sweet **comedy**. No more words: away! go; away!

[Exeunt.]

Italian

actors: attori.
apparel: vestimento, abito.
beards: barbe.
breath: alito, respiro, fiato, soffio.
clean: pulito, pulire, puliamo, pulite, puliscono, pulisco, pulisci, puro, netto, lindo.
comedy: commedia.
dear: caro, costoso, egregio.
dined: pranzato, cenato.
doubt: dubitare, dubbio.
duke: duca.

eat: mangiare, mangi, mangia, mangiamo, mangiano, mangiate, mangio.
hang: pendere, appendere, sospendere, impiccare.
hear: udire, odono, odi, odo, udite, udiamo, sentire, sentono, sento, sentite, senti.
linen: lino, biancheria.
lion: leone.
nails: chiodi.
nor: ne.

palace: palazzo, il palazzo.
pare: pelare.
plays: gioca, suona.
preferred: preferito.
presently: attualmente.
pumps: pompe.
short: corto, breve, basso.
sweet: dolce, soave, caramella.
utter: totale, completo, proferire, emettere.
word: parola, vocabolo, termine, verbo, formulare.

ACT V

SCENE I. **ATHENS**.
AN APARTMENT IN THE PALACE OF THESEUS.

[Enter THESEUS, HIPPOLYTA, PHILOSTRATE, Lords, and Attendants.]
HIPPOLYTA
> 'Tis **strange**, my Theseus, that these **lovers speak** of.

THESEUS
> More strange than **true**. I never may believe
> These **antique** fables, **nor** these **fairy** toys.
> Lovers and **madmen** have such **seething** brains,
> Such **shaping** fantasies, that apprehend
> More than **cool reason** ever comprehends.
> The **lunatic**, the lover, and the poet
> Are of **imagination** all compact:
> One **sees** more devils than **vast hell** can hold;
> That is the **madman**: the lover, all as frantic,
> Sees Helen's **beauty** in a **brow** of Egypt:
> The poet's **eye**, in a **fine frenzy** rolling,

Italian

antique: antico.
athens: Atene.
beauty: bellezza.
brow: sopracciglio, fronte.
cool: fresco, raffreddare, freddo.
eye: occhio, cruna.
fairy: fata.
fine: multa, contravvenzione, multare, bello, delicato, carino, eccellente, penale, ammenda.
frenzy: frenesia.
hell: inferno.

imagination: immagine, immaginazione, fantasia.
lover: amante.
lunatic: pazzo, lunatico.
madman: pazzo.
madmen: pazzi.
nor: ne.
reason: ragione, causa, intelletto, ragionare, argomentare, motivo.
sees: vede, sega.
seething: bollendo, ribollendo.
shaping: sagomatura.

speak: parlare, parla, parlo, parliamo, parli, parlate, parlano, favellare.
strange: strano.
true: vero.
vast: vasto.

Doth **glance** from **heaven** to earth, from earth to heaven;
And as **imagination** bodies forth
The **forms** of things **unknown**, the poet's pen
Turns them to shapes, and gives to **airy** nothing
A local **habitation** and a name.
Such tricks hath **strong** imagination,
That, if it would but **apprehend** some **joy**,
It **comprehends** some bringer of that joy;
Or in the night, **imagining** some fear,
How **easy** is a **bush supposed** a bear?

HIPPOLYTA

But all the story of the night told over,
And all their minds transfigur'd so together,
More witnesseth than fancy's images,
And **grows** to something of great constancy;
But, **howsoever**, strange and admirable.

[Enter LYSANDER, DEMETRIUS, HERMIA, and HELENA.]

THESEUS

Here come the lovers, full of joy and mirth.--
Joy, **gentle** friends! joy and fresh days of love
Accompany your **hearts**!

LYSANDER

                     More than to us
Wait in your **royal walks**, your **board**, your bed!

THESEUS

Come now; what masques, what dances shall we have,
To **wear** away this long age of three hours
Between our after-supper and bed-time?
Where is our **usual manager** of mirth?
What revels are in hand? Is there no play

Italian

airy: arioso.
apprehend: capiamo, capisci, capisco, capiscono, capite, temono, comprendono, temete, comprendi, afferro, temo.
board: consiglio, asse, tavola, commissione, bordo, scheda, pannello.
bush: arbusto, cespuglio, boccola, bussola.
comprehends: comprende.
easy: facile, semplice.

forms: moduli.
gentle: mite, gentile, dolce, delicato.
glance: occhiata, sguardo.
grows: cresce, coltiva.
habitation: abitazione.
hearts: cuori.
heaven: cielo, paradiso.
howsoever: comunque.
imagination: immagine, immaginazione, fantasia.
imagining: immaginando.
joy: gioia.

manager: direttore, amministratore, manager, gestore, gerente, dirigente, amministratore delegato.
royal: reale.
strong: forte, robusto.
supposed: supposto.
unknown: sconosciuto, ignoto.
usual: usuale, consueto, solito, generale, abituale.
walks: cammina.
wear: portare, usura, logoramento, indossare.

To **ease** the **anguish** of a **torturing** hour?
Call Philostrate.

PHILOSTRATE
                    Here, **mighty** Theseus.

THESEUS
Say, what **abridgment** have you for this evening?
What masque? what music? How shall we beguile
The **lazy** time, if not with some **delight**?

PHILOSTRATE
There is a **brief** how many **sports** are ripe;
Make **choice** of which your **highness** will see first.
[Giving a paper.]

THESEUS
[Reads.]
        'The battle with the Centaurs, to be sung
        By an Athenian **eunuch** to the harp.'
We'll none of that: that have I told my love,
In **glory** of my **kinsman** Hercules.
        'The **riot** of the **tipsy** Bacchanals,
        Tearing the Thracian **singer** in their rage.'
That is an old **device**, and it was play'd
When I from Thebes came last a conqueror.
        'The **thrice** three Muses **mourning** for the death
        Of **learning**, late deceas'd in beggary.'
That is some **satire**, keen and critical,
Not **sorting** with a **nuptial** ceremony.
        'A **tedious** brief scene of young Pyramus
        And his love Thisbe; very **tragical** mirth.'
Merry and tragical! tedious and brief!
That is hot ice and **wondrous** strange snow.
How shall we find the **concord** of this **discord**?

Italian

abridgment: compendio.
anguish: angoscia.
brief: breve, corto, riassunto, conciso, memoria.
concord: accordo.
delight: delizia, deliziare, dilettare, diletto, godimento, rallegrare, gioia.
device: dispositivo, apparecchio, congegno.
discord: disaccordo.
ease: agio, facilità.
eunuch: eunuco.

glory: gloria.
highness: altezza.
ice: ghiaccio, glassare.
kinsman: parente.
lazy: pigro, indolente.
learning: imparando, apprendimento.
mighty: poderoso, forte, possente, potente.
mourning: lutto, piangendo.
nuptial: nuziale.
riot: sommossa, tumulto, rivolta, tumultuare.

satire: satira.
singer: cantante.
sorting: smistamento, cernita, classificazione, ordinamento.
sports: sport, sportivo.
tedious: noioso, tedioso.
thrice: tre volte.
tipsy: alticcio.
torturing: torturare.
tragical: tragico.
wondrous: meraviglioso.

PHILOSTRATE

A **play** there is, my **lord**, some ten **words** long,
Which is as **brief** as I have known a play;
But by ten words, my lord, it is too long,
Which **makes** it **tedious**: for in all the play
There is not one word **apt**, one **player** fitted:
And **tragical**, my **noble** lord, it is;
For Pyramus **therein** doth **kill** himself:
Which when I saw **rehears'd**, I must confess,
Made **mine** eyes water; but more **merry** tears
The **passion** of **loud laughter** never shed.

THESEUS

What are they that do play it?

PHILOSTRATE

Hard-handed men that work in Athens here,
Which never labour'd in their minds **till** now;
And now have toil'd their unbreath'd memories
With this same play against your **nuptial**.

THESEUS

And we will hear it.

PHILOSTRATE

              No, my noble lord,
It is not for you: I have **heard** it over,
And it is nothing, nothing in the world;
Unless you can find **sport** in their intents,
Extremely stretch'd and conn'd with **cruel** pain,
To do you service.

THESEUS

            I will hear that play;
For never anything can be **amiss**

Italian

amiss: male, inopportuno.
apt: adatto.
brief: breve, corto, riassunto, conciso, memoria.
cruel: crudele.
hear: udire, odono, odi, odo, udite, udiamo, sentire, sentono, sento, sentite, senti.
heard: udito, sentito.
kill: uccidere, ammazzare.
laughter: risa, risata, riso.
lord: signore.

loud: forte, alto, rumoroso.
makes: fa, commette.
merry: allegro, festoso, gaio.
mine: miniera, mina, minare, estrarre.
noble: nobile, gentilizio, nobiliare.
nuptial: nuziale.
passion: ardore, passione.
play: giocare, giocano, giocate, giochiamo, gioca, giochi, gioco, suonare, suona, suoni, suoniamo.
player: giocatore.
sport: sport.

tedious: noioso, tedioso.
therein: in ciò.
till: finchè, coltivare, cassa, fino, arare.
tragical: tragico.
word: parola, vocabolo, termine, verbo, formulare.

When **simpleness** and **duty tender** it.
Go, bring them in: and take your places, ladies.

[Exit PHILOSTRATE.]

HIPPOLYTA

I love not to see wretchedness o'er-charged,
And duty in his service **perishing**.

THESEUS

Why, **gentle sweet**, you shall see no such thing.

HIPPOLYTA

He says they can do nothing in this kind.

THESEUS

The kinder we, to give them **thanks** for nothing.
Our **sport** shall be to take what they mistake:
And what poor duty **cannot** do,
Noble **respect** takes it in might, not merit.
Where I have come, great clerks have purposed
To **greet** me with **premeditated welcomes**;
Where I have seen them **shiver** and look pale,
Make periods in the **midst** of sentences,
Throttle their practis'd **accent** in their fears,
And, in **conclusion**, **dumbly** have **broke** off,
Not **paying** me a welcome. Trust me, sweet,
Out of this **silence** yet I pick'd a welcome;
And in the **modesty** of **fearful** duty
I read as much as from the rattling tongue
Of **saucy** and **audacious** eloquence.
Love, therefore, and tongue-tied simplicity
In **least** speak most to my **capacity**.

[**Enter** PHILOSTRATE.]

Italian

accent: accento, accentare, accentano, accentate, accenti, accentiamo, accenta.
audacious: audace.
broke: al verde, rovinato, scarti di fabbricazione.
cannot: non potere.
capacity: capacità, capienza.
conclusion: conclusione, risultato.
dumbly: mutamente.
duty: dovere, dazio, imposta, mansione.

enter: entrare, entra, entrano, entrate, entri, entriamo, entro, invio.
fearful: spaventoso, pauroso.
gentle: mite, gentile, dolce, delicato.
greet: salutare, saluti, salutiamo, salutate, salutano, saluta, saluto.
least: minimo, meno.
midst: mezzo.
modesty: modestia, verecondia.
paying: pagando.
perishing: perendo.
premeditated: premeditato.

respect: rispettare, rispetto, stima.
saucy: impertinente, sfacciato.
shiver: tremare, brivido, rabbrividire.
silence: silenzio.
simpleness: semplicità.
sport: sport.
sweet: dolce, soave, caramella.
tender: tenero, dolce, offerta, tender.
thanks: grazie, ringrazia.
welcome: benvenuto, bene arrivate, accoglienza, gradito, accogliere.

PHILOSTRATE

So please your **grace**, the **prologue** is address'd.

THESEUS

Let him approach.

[**Flourish** of trumpets. **Enter** PROLOGUE.]

PROLOGUE

'If we **offend**, it is with our good will.
That you should think, we come not to offend,
But with good will. To show our simple skill,
That is the true **beginning** of our end.
Consider then, we come but in despite.
We do not come, as minding to **content** you,
Our true **intent** is. All for your delight
We are not here. That you should here **repent** you,
The **actors** are at hand: and, by their show,
You shall know all that you are like to know,'

THESEUS

This **fellow** doth not stand upon **points**.

LYSANDER

He hath **rid** his prologue like a **rough colt**; he **knows** not the **stop**. A good
moral, my lord: it is not enough to speak, but to speak true.

HIPPOLYTA

Indeed he hath played on this prologue like a child on a **recorder**; a sound,
but not in government.

THESEUS

His **speech** was like a **tangled chain**; nothing **impaired**, but all disordered.
Who is next?

[Enter PYRAMUS and THISBE, WALL, MOONSHINE, and LION, as in
dumb show.]

Italian

actors: attori.
beginning: inizio, cominciando, principio, iniziando.
chain: catena, catenina.
colt: puledro.
content: contenuto, contento, soddisfatto, soddisfare.
dumb: muto.
enter: entrare, entra, entrano, entrate, entri, entriamo, entro, invio.
fellow: uomo.
flourish: fiorire, fiorisci, fiorisco,

fioriscono, fiorite, fioriamo, prosperare.
grace: grazia.
impaired: danneggiato.
intent: intento, intenzione.
knows: conosce, sa.
moral: morale.
offend: offendere, offendiamo, offendo, offendi, offendete, offendono, insultare, insulto, insulti, insultate, insultano.
points: punti, scambio.

prologue: prologo.
recorder: registratore, flauto dolce.
repent: pentirsi.
rid: sbarazzare.
rough: rude, brusco, ruvido, crudo, approssimativo, rozzo, grossolano, scabro, grezzo.
speech: discorso, orazione, parola.
stop: fermare, ferma, fermarsi, fermo, fermi, fermate, fermano, fermiamo, fermata, cessare, cesso.
tangled: aggrovigliato.

PROLOGUE

Gentles,   perchance you **wonder** at this show;
But wonder on, **till** truth make all things plain.
This man is Pyramus, if you would know;
This beauteous lady Thisby is certain.
This man, with **lime** and rough-cast, doth present
Wall, that **vile** Wall which did these lovers sunder;
And through Wall's **chink**, poor souls, they are content
To **whisper**, at the which let no man wonder.
This man, with lanthorn, dog, and **bush** of thorn,
Presenteth Moonshine: for, if you will know,
By **moonshine** did these lovers think no scorn
To meet at Ninus' **tomb**, there, there to woo.
This **grisly beast**, which by name Lion hight,
The **trusty** Thisby, coming first by night,
Did **scare** away, or rather did affright;
And as she **fled**, her **mantle** she did fall;
Which Lion vile with **bloody** mouth did stain:
Anon comes Pyramus, **sweet youth**, and tall,
And **finds** his trusty Thisby's mantle slain;
Whereat with **blade**, with bloody **blameful** blade,
He **bravely** broach'd his **boiling** bloody breast;
And Thisby, **tarrying** in **mulberry** shade,
His **dagger** drew, and **died**. For all the rest,
Let Lion, Moonshine, Wall, and lovers twain,
At large **discourse** while here they do remain.

[Exeunt PROLOGUE, THISBE, LION, and MOONSHINE.]

THESEUS

I wonder if the **lion** be to speak.

DEMETRIUS

No wonder, my lord: one lion may, when many asses do.

Italian

beast: bestia, animale.
blade: spada, pala, lametta, lama.
blameful: biasimevole, riprovevole.
bloody: sanguinante, sanguinoso, maledetto, cruento.
boiling: bollente, ebollizione, bollitura, bollire.
bravely: coraggiosamente.
bush: arbusto, cespuglio, boccola, bussola.
chink: fessura.
dagger: pugnale, daga.

died: morto.
discourse: discorso.
finds: fonde, fonda.
fled: fuggito.
grisly: spiacevole, sgradevole, orribile.
lime: calce, lime.
lion: leone.
mantle: mantello, manto.
moonshine: chiaro di luna.
mulberry: gelso.
scare: spaventare, impaurire, spavento.

sweet: dolce, soave, caramella.
tarrying: rimanendo.
till: finchè, coltivare, cassa, fino, arare.
tomb: tomba, sepolcro.
trusty: fedele, fidato.
vile: abietto.
whisper: sussurrare, bisbigliare, bisbiglio.
wonder: stupirsi, stupore, meraviglia, domandarsi, meravigliarsi.
youth: gioventù, giovinezza, adolescenza, giovane.

WALL

In this same **interlude** it doth befall
That I, one Snout by name, present a wall:
And such a wall as I would have you think
That had in it a crannied **hole** or **chink**,
Through which the lovers, Pyramus and Thisby,
Did **whisper** often very secretly.
This **loam**, this rough-cast, and this **stone**, doth show
That I am that same wall; the truth is so:
And this the **cranny** is, right and sinister,
Through which the **fearful** lovers are to whisper.

THESEUS

Would you **desire lime** and hair to speak better?

DEMETRIUS

It is the wittiest **partition** that ever I heard
discourse, my lord.

THESEUS

Pyramus **draws** near the wall; **silence**.

[**Enter** PYRAMUS.]

PYRAMUS

O grim-look'd night! O night with **hue** so black!
O night, which ever art when day is not!
O night, O night, alack, alack, alack,
I fear my Thisby's **promise** is forgot!--
And **thou**, O wall, O **sweet**, O **lovely** wall,
That stand'st between her father's ground and **mine**;
Thou wall, O wall, O sweet and lovely wall,
 Show me **thy** chink, to **blink** through with mine eyne.

[WALL holds up his fingers.]

Thanks, **courteous** wall: Jove **shield thee** well for this!
But what see what see I? No Thisby do I see.

Italian

blink: lampeggiare, ammiccare.
chink: fessura.
courteous: cortese.
cranny: fessura, crepa.
desire: desiderio, desiderare, bramare.
draws: disegna.
enter: entrare, entra, entrano, entrate, entri, entriamo, entro, invio.
fearful: spaventoso, pauroso.
hole: buco, foro, apertura, forare, buca, bucare.
hue: tinta.

interlude: intermezzo, interludio, intervallo.
lime: calce, lime.
loam: argilla.
lovely: bello, piacevole, amabile, grazioso, gradevole, affascinante, caro, carino.
mine: miniera, mina, minare, estrarre.
partition: partizione, parete divisoria, tramezzo.
promise: promessa, promettere, promettono, promettete, prometti,

promettiamo, prometto.
shield: scudo, riparo, proteggere, schermo, schermare.
silence: silenzio.
stone: pietra, calcolo, sasso, la pietra, ciottolo.
sweet: dolce, soave, caramella.
thee: te.
thou: tu.
thy: tuo.
whisper: sussurrare, bisbigliare, bisbiglio.

O **wicked wall**, through **whom** I see no bliss,
Curs'd be **thy** stones for thus **deceiving** me!

THESEUS

The wall, methinks, being **sensible**, should **curse** again.

PYRAMUS

No, in **truth**, sir, he should not. 'Deceiving me' is Thisby's **cue**: she is to **enter** now, and I am to **spy** her through the wall. You shall see it will **fall pat** as I told you. — Yonder she comes.

[Enter THISBE.]

THISBE

O wall, full often hast **thou** heard my moans,
For **parting** my **fair** Pyramus and me:
My **cherry** lips have often kiss'd thy stones:
Thy stones with **lime** and hair **knit** up in **thee**.

PYRAMUS

I see a voice; now will I to the chink,
To spy an I can hear my Thisby's face.
Thisby!

THISBE

My love! thou art my love, I think.

PYRAMUS

Think what thou **wilt**, I am thy lover's grace;
And like Limander am I **trusty still**.

THISBE

And I like Helen, till the fates me **kill**.

PYRAMUS

Not Shafalus to Procrus was so true.

THISBE

As Shafalus to Procrus, I to you.

Italian

cherry: ciliegia.
cue: stecca.
curse: bestemmiare, maledire, imprecare, maledizione, imprecazione.
deceiving: ingannando, truffando, ingannare.
enter: entrare, entra, entrano, entrate, entri, entriamo, entro, invio.
fair: biondo, fiera, giusto, bazar, correttamente, bello, equo.
fall: cadere, caduta, autunno, cadono,

cado, cadiamo, cadi, cadete, diminuire, calo, piombare.
kill: uccidere, ammazzare.
knit: lavorare a maglia, aggrottare.
lime: calce, lime.
parting: separazione, divisione.
pat: colpetto.
sensible: sensato, ragionevole, sensibile.
spy: spiare, spia.
thee: te.
thou: tu.

thy: tuo.
till: finchè, coltivare, cassa, fino, arare.
trusty: fedele, fidato.
truth: verità.
wall: muro, parete.
whom: chi, cui.
wicked: cattivo, malvagio.
wilt: appassire, appassisco, appassiscono, appassisci, appassiamo, appassite.

PYRAMUS
O, **kiss** me through the **hole** of this **vile wall**.

THISBE
I kiss the wall's hole, not your lips at all.

PYRAMUS
Wilt **thou** at Ninny's **tomb** meet me straightway?

THISBE
'Tide life, 'tide death, I come without **delay**.

WALL
Thus have I, wall, my part **discharged** so;
And, being done, thus Wall away doth go.

[Exeunt WALL, PYRAMUS and THISBE.]

THESEUS
Now is the **mural** down between the two neighbours.

DEMETRIUS
No **remedy**, my lord, when walls are so **wilful** to hear without **warning**.

HIPPOLYTA
This is the silliest **stuff** that ever I heard.

THESEUS
The best in this kind are but shadows; and the worst
are no **worse**, if **imagination amend** them.

HIPPOLYTA
It must be your imagination then, and not **theirs**.

THESEUS
If we **imagine** no worse of them than they of
themselves, they may **pass** for **excellent** men.
Here come two **noble** beasts in, a **moon** and a **lion**.

[**Enter** LION and MOONSHINE.]

Italian

amend: emendare, emendo, emendiamo, emendi, emendate, emendano, emenda.
delay: ritardo, tardare, ritardare, indugio, indugiare.
discharged: scaricato.
enter: entrare, entra, entrano, entrate, entri, entriamo, entro, invio.
excellent: eccellente, esimio, ottimo.
hole: buco, foro, apertura, forare, buca, bucare.
imagination: immagine, immaginazione, fantasia.
imagine: immaginare, figurarsi, immagino, immaginiamo, immagini, immaginano, immaginate, immagina.
kiss: bacio, baciare, baciarsi.
lion: leone.
moon: luna, la luna.
mural: murale.
noble: nobile, gentilizio, nobiliare.
pass: passare, passaggio, lasciapassare, passata, trascorrere, passo.
remedy: rimedio, medicina, rimediare.
stuff: materiale, farcire, roba, imbottire.
theirs: loro.
thou: tu.
tomb: tomba, sepolcro.
vile: abietto.
wall: muro, parete.
warning: avvertendo, avviso, avvertimento, diffida, avvertenza.
wilful: intenzionale, testardo.
worse: peggiore, peggio.

LION

> You, **ladies**, you, whose **gentle hearts** do fear
> The smallest **monstrous mouse** that **creeps** on floor,
> May now, **perchance**, both **quake** and **tremble** here,
> When **lion rough** in wildest **rage** doth roar.
> Then know that I, one Snug the **joiner**, am
> A lion **fell**, **nor** else no lion's dam:
> For, if I should as lion come in strife
> Into this place, 'twere **pity** on my life.

THESEUS

> A very gentle **beast**, and of a good **conscience**.

DEMETRIUS

> The very best at a beast, my **lord**, that e'er I saw.

LYSANDER

> This lion is a very **fox** for his **valour**.

THESEUS

> True; and a **goose** for his **discretion**.

DEMETRIUS

> Not so, my lord; for his valour **cannot carry** his
> discretion, and the fox **carries** the goose.

THESEUS

> His discretion, I am sure, cannot carry his valour;
> for the goose carries not the fox. It is well; leave it to his
> discretion, and let us **listen** to the **moon**.

MOONSHINE

> This lanthorn doth the **horned** moon present:

DEMETRIUS

> He should have **worn** the horns on his head.

Italian

beast: bestia, animale.
cannot: non potere.
carries: porta, trasporta.
carry: portare, porti, portate, portiamo, portano, porto, porta, trasportare, trasporta, trasportano, trasportate.
conscience: coscienza.
creeps: striscia.
discretion: discrezione.
fell: abbattere.
fox: volpe, la volpe.
gentle: mite, gentile, dolce, delicato.

goose: oca, l'oca.
hearts: cuori.
horned: cornuto.
joiner: falegname.
ladies: signore.
lion: leone.
listen: ascoltare, ascolti, ascoltiamo, ascoltate, ascoltano, ascolta, ascolto.
lord: signore.
monstrous: mostruoso.
moon: luna, la luna.
mouse: topo, sorcio, mouse, il topo.

nor: ne.
perchance: forse.
pity: compassione, pietà.
quake: tremito, tremare.
rage: furore, ira, furia, collera.
rough: rude, brusco, ruvido, crudo, approssimativo, rozzo, grossolano, scabro, grezzo.
tremble: tremare.
valour: valore.
worn: consumato, usato, esausto, portato, logoro.

THESEUS

He is no **crescent**, and his horns are **invisible** within
the circumference.

MOONSHINE

This lanthorn doth the **horned moon** present;
Myself the man i' the moon do **seem** to be.

THESEUS

This is the greatest **error** of all the **rest**: the man should be
put into the **lantern**. How is it else the man i' the moon?

DEMETRIUS

He **dares** not come there for the **candle**: for, you
see, it is already in **snuff**.

HIPPOLYTA

I am aweary of this moon: would he would change!

THESEUS

It **appears**, by his small **light** of **discretion**, that he
is in the **wane**: but yet, in **courtesy**, in all **reason**, we must
stay the time.

LYSANDER

Proceed, moon.

MOON

All that I have to say, is to tell you that the lantern
is the moon; I, the man i' the moon; this thorn-bush, my
thorn-bush; and this **dog**, my dog.

DEMETRIUS

Why, all these should be in the lantern; for all
these are in the moon. But **silence**; here **comes** Thisbe.

[**Enter** THISBE.]

Italian

appears: appare.
candle: candela, la candela, cero.
comes: viene.
courtesy: cortesia.
crescent: mezzaluna.
dares: osa.
discretion: discrezione.
dog: cane, il cane.
enter: entrare, entra, entrano, entrate,
  entri, entriamo, entro, invio.
error: errore, sbaglio, fallo.
horned: cornuto.

invisible: invisibile.
lantern: lanterna.
light: luce, leggero, accendere, chiaro,
  illuminare, fanale, lampada,
  luminoso, debole.
moon: luna, la luna.
reason: ragione, causa, intelletto,
  ragionare, argomentare, motivo.
rest: riposo, riposarsi, riposare, resto,
  pausa.
seem: parere, paiono, paiamo, pari,
  paio, parete, sembrare, sembra,

sembrano, sembrate, sembri.
silence: silenzio.
snuff: tabacco da fiuto.
wane: declinare, declino, declina,
  declinano, declinate, declini,
  decliniamo.

THISBE
> This is old Ninny's **tomb**. Where is my love?

LION
> Oh!

[The LION roars.--THISBE **runs** off.]

DEMETRIUS
> Well roared, **lion**.

THESEUS
> Well run, Thisbe.

HIPPOLYTA
> Well shone, **moon**.--Truly, the moon shines with a good **grace**.

[The LION **tears** THISBE'S Mantle, and exit.]

THESEUS
> Well moused, lion.

DEMETRIUS
> And so **comes** Pyramus.

LYSANDER
> And then the lion **vanishes**.

[**Enter** PYRAMUS.]

PYRAMUS
> Sweet moon, I **thank thee** for **thy sunny** beams;
> I thank thee, moon, for **shining** now so bright:
> For, by thy **gracious golden**, **glittering** streams,
> I **trust** to take of truest Thisby's sight.
> > But stay;--O spite!
> > But mark,--poor knight,
> > What **dreadful dole** is here!
> > Eyes, do you see?
> > How can it be?

Italian

comes: viene.
dole: sussidio.
dreadful: terribile.
enter: entrare, entra, entrano, entrate, entri, entriamo, entro, invio.
glittering: scintillare, brillio, brillare, scintillio.
golden: dorato, aureo, d'oro.
grace: grazia.
gracious: grazioso.
lion: leone.
moon: luna, la luna.

runs: corre, scorre.
shining: lucente, brillante.
sunny: soleggiato, assolato.
tears: lacrime.
thank: ringraziare, ringraziano, ringraziate, ringraziamo, ringrazia, ringrazi, ringrazio.
thee: te.
thy: tuo.
tomb: tomba, sepolcro.
trust: fiducia, trust, confidenza, affidamento.

vanishes: sparisce.

O **dainty duck**! O **dear**!
Thy **mantle** good,
What! **stained** with blood?
Approach, **ye** furies fell!
O fates! come, come;
Cut **thread** and thrum;
Quail, **rush**, **conclude**, and **quell**!

THESEUS

This **passion**, and the death of a dear **friend**, would go
near to make a man look sad.

HIPPOLYTA

Beshrew my **heart**, but I **pity** the man.

PYRAMUS

O **wherefore**, **nature**, didst **thou lions** frame?
Since lion **vile** hath here deflower'd my dear;
Which is--no, no--which was the fairest dame
That liv'd, that lov'd, that lik'd, that look'd with cheer.
Come, **tears**, confound;
Out, **sword**, and wound
The **pap** of Pyramus:
Ay, that left pap,
Where heart doth hop:--
Thus **die** I, thus, thus, thus.
Now am I dead,
Now am I fled;
My **soul** is in the sky:
Tongue, **lose thy** light!
Moon, take thy flight!
Now die, die, die, die, die.
[Dies. **Exit** MOONSHINE.]

Italian

conclude: concludere, concludo, concludono, concludiamo, concludi, concludete.
dainty: delicato.
dear: caro, costoso, egregio.
die: morire, muoio, muori, muoiono, morite, moriamo, dado, cubo, matrice, stampo.
duck: anatra, anitra, l'anatra.
exit: uscita, uscire, l'uscita.
friend: amico, amica.
heart: cuore, il cuore.

lion: leone.
lose: perdere, perdiamo, perdete, perdi, perdo, perdono.
mantle: mantello, manto.
nature: natura, indole, carattere.
pap: pappa.
passion: ardore, passione.
pity: compassione, pietà.
quell: soffocare, soffochi, soffochiamo, soffocate, soffocano, soffoca, soffoco.
rush: affrettarsi, giunco, furia.
soul: anima.

stained: macchiato.
sword: spada.
tears: lacrime.
thou: tu.
thread: filo, filetto, filettatura.
thy: tuo.
vile: abietto.
wherefore: perchè.
ye: voi, tu.

DEMETRIUS
No **die**, but an **ace**, for him; for he is but one.

LYSANDER
Less than an ace, man; for he is **dead**; he is nothing.

THESEUS
With the help of a **surgeon** he might yet **recover** and **prove** an **ass**.

HIPPOLYTA
How **chance moonshine** is gone before Thisbe **comes** back and **finds** her **lover**?

THESEUS
She will find him by starlight.--Here she comes; and her **passion** ends the play.

[**Enter** THISBE.]

HIPPOLYTA
Methinks she should not use a long one for such a Pyramus: I hope she will be **brief**.

DEMETRIUS
A mote will turn the **balance**, which Pyramus, which Thisbe, is the better.

LYSANDER
She hath spied him already with those **sweet** eyes.

DEMETRIUS
And thus she moans, videlicet.--

THISBE
> Asleep, my love?
> What, dead, my dove?
> O Pyramus, arise,
> Speak, **speak**. Quite dumb?
> Dead, dead? A tomb
> Must cover **thy** sweet eyes.

Italian

ace: asso.
ass: asino, ciuco, somaro, culo.
balance: equilibrio, saldo, bilancio, bilanciamento, bilanciare, equilibrare, bilancia, quadrare, pareggio.
brief: breve, corto, riassunto, conciso, memoria.
chance: caso.
comes: viene.
cover: coprire, coperta, copertura, copertina, percorrere, coperchio, legatura.

dead: morto.
die: morire, muoio, muori, muoiono, morite, moriamo, dado, cubo, matrice, stampo.
enter: entrare, entra, entrano, entrate, entri, entriamo, entro, invio.
finds: fonde, fonda.
lover: amante.
moonshine: chiaro di luna.
passion: ardore, passione.
prove: provare, proviamo, provi, provate, provano, provo, prova,

comprovare, dimostrare.
recover: ricuperare, ricupera, ricuperi, ricuperiamo, ricuperano, ricuperate, ricupero, recuperare, guarire, riprendere.
speak: parlare, parla, parlo, parliamo, parli, parlate, parlano, favellare.
surgeon: chirurgo.
sweet: dolce, soave, caramella.
thy: tuo.

These lily lips,
This **cherry** nose,
These **yellow cowslip** cheeks,
Are gone, are gone:
Lovers, make moan!
His eyes were **green** as leeks.
O Sisters Three,
Come, come to me,
With hands as **pale** as milk;
Lay them in gore,
Since you have shore
With **shears** his **thread** of silk.
Tongue, not a word:--
Come, **trusty** sword;
Come, **blade**, my **breast** imbrue;
And **farewell**, friends:--
Thus Thisbe ends;
Adieu, **adieu**, adieu.

[Dies.]

THESEUS

Moonshine and **lion** are left to **bury** the **dead**.

DEMETRIUS

Ay, and **wall** too.

BOTTOM

No, I **assure** you; the wall is down that parted their fathers. Will it please you
to see the **epilogue**, or to hear a Bergomask **dance** between two of our
company?

THESEUS

No epilogue, I **pray** you; for your play needs no **excuse**. Never excuse; for
when the players are all dead there need **none** to be blamed. **Marry**, if he that
writ it had **played** Pyramus, and hang'd himself in Thisbe's **garter**, it would

Italian

adieu: addio.

assure: assicurare, assicura,
  assicuriamo, assicurate, assicuri,
  assicurano, assicuro, garantire.

blade: spada, pala, lametta, lama.

breast: petto, seno, mammella.

bury: seppellire, seppelliamo,
  seppellisci, seppellisco,
  seppelliscono, seppellite, sotterrare.

cherry: ciliegia.

cowslip: primula.

dance: ballare, ballo, danza.

dead: morto.

epilogue: epilogo.

excuse: scusa, scusare, giustificazione,
  pretesto.

farewell: addio, congedo.

garter: giarrettiera.

green: verde, acerbo.

lion: leone.

marry: sposare, sposati, sposatevi, si
  sposi, si sposate, si sposano, ci
  sposiamo, mi sposo, maritarsi,
  ammogliarsi, maritare.

none: nessuno.

pale: pallido, smorto, impallidire.

played: giocato, suonato.

pray: pregare, pregate, prego, preghi,
  prega, preghiamo, pregano.

shears: forbici, cesoia.

thread: filo, filetto, filettatura.

trusty: fedele, fidato.

wall: muro, parete.

writ: documento, mandato.

yellow: giallo.

have been a **fine tragedy**: and so it is, **truly**; and very **notably discharged**.
But come, your Bergomask; let your **epilogue** alone.
[Here a **dance** of Clowns.]
The **iron tongue** of **midnight** hath told twelve:--
Lovers, to bed; 'tis almost **fairy** time.
I **fear** we shall out-sleep the coming morn,
As much as we this night have overwatch'd.
This palpable-gross play hath well beguil'd
The **heavy gait** of night.--Sweet **friends**, to bed.--
A **fortnight hold** we this solemnity,
In **nightly** revels and new jollity.

[Exeunt.]

SCENE II

[Enter PUCK.]

PUCK

　　　Now the **hungry lion** roars,
　　　And the **wolf** behowls the moon;
　　　Whilst the heavy **ploughman** snores,
　　　All with **weary task** fordone.
　　　Now the **wasted** brands do glow,
　　　Whilst the scritch-owl, scritching loud,
　　　Puts the **wretch** that lies in woe
　　　In **remembrance** of a shroud.
　　　Now it is the time of night
　　　That the **graves**, all gaping wide,
　　　Every one **lets forth** its sprite,
　　　In the church-way **paths** to glide:

Italian

dance: ballare, ballo, danza.
discharged: scaricato.
epilogue: epilogo.
fairy: fata.
fear: paura, temere, angoscia, timore, aver timore.
fine: multa, contravvenzione, multare, bello, delicato, carino, eccellente, penale, ammenda.
forth: avanti.
fortnight: due settimane.
friends: amici.

gait: andatura.
graves: tombe.
heavy: pesante, grave.
hold: tenere, stiva, stretta, mantenere, ritenere.
hungry: affamato.
iron: ferro, ferro da stiro, stirare.
lets: affitta.
lion: leone.
midnight: mezzanotte.
nightly: di ogni notte, ogni notte.
notably: notevolmente.

paths: percorsi.
ploughman: aratore.
remembrance: rimembranza, ricordo, memoria.
task: compito, lavoro, incarico.
tongue: lingua, linguetta, la lingua.
tragedy: tragedia.
truly: davvero, infatti, veramente.
wasted: sprecato.
weary: stanco, stancare, fiacco.
wolf: lupo.
wretch: sciagurato.

And we fairies, that do run
By the **triple** Hecate's team
From the **presence** of the sun,
Following **darkness** like a dream,
Now are **frolic**; not a mouse
Shall **disturb** this hallow'd house:
I am **sent** with **broom** before,
To **sweep** the **dust** behind the door.

[Enter OBERON and TITANIA, with their Train.]

OBERON

Through the house give glimmering light,
By the **dead** and **drowsy** fire:
Every **elf** and **fairy** sprite
Hop as light as **bird** from brier:
And this ditty, after me,
Sing and **dance** it trippingly.

TITANIA

First, **rehearse** your **song** by rote,
To each word a warbling note;
Hand in hand, with fairy grace,
Will we **sing**, and **bless** this place.

[Song and Dance.]

OBERON

Now, until the **break** of day,
Through this house each fairy stray,
To the best bride-bed will we,
Which by us shall **blessed** be;
And the **issue** there create
Ever shall be fortunate.
So shall all the **couples** three
Ever true in **loving** be;

Italian

bird: uccello, l'uccello.
bless: benedire, benedi', benedite, benedicono, benedico, benedici, benediciamo.
blessed: benedetto, beato.
break: rompere, rottura, spezzare, rompersi, frattura, pausa, schiantare, infrangere, sosta, spaccare.
broom: scopa, granata, ginestra, la scopa.
couples: coppia.
dance: ballare, ballo, danza.

darkness: oscurità, tenebre.
dead: morto.
disturb: disturbare, disturbiamo, disturba, disturbano, disturbate, disturbi, disturbo.
drowsy: sonnolento.
dust: polvere, spolverare.
elf: elfo.
fairy: fata.
frolic: cattivo.
issue: pubblicare, emissione, problema, emettere, proclamare,

prole, rilasciare, fascicolo, discendenza, uscita.
loving: affettuoso.
presence: presenza.
rehearse: proviamo, provo, provi, provate, provano, provare, prova.
sent: mandato, spedito.
sing: cantare, canta, cantano, cantate, canti, cantiamo, canto.
song: canzone, canto.
sweep: spazzare, scopare, spazzata.
triple: triplo.

And the blots of Nature's hand
Shall not in their **issue** stand:
Never **mole**, **hare**-lip, **nor** scar,
Nor **mark prodigious**, such as are
Despised in nativity,
Shall upon their children be.--
With this field-dew consecrate,
Every **fairy** take his gate;
And each several **chamber** bless,
Through this **palace**, with **sweet** peace;
E'er shall it in **safety** rest,
And the **owner** of it blest.
Trip away:
Make no stay:
Meet me all by **break** of day.

[Exeunt OBERON, TITANIA, and Train.]

PUCK

If we shadows have offended,
Think but this,--and all is mended,--
That you have but slumber'd here
While these visions did appear.
And this **weak** and **idle** theme,
No more **yielding** but a dream,
Gentles, do not reprehend;
If you **pardon**, we will mend.
And, as I am an **honest** Puck,
If we have **unearned** luck
Now to 'scape the serpent's tongue,
We will make **amends** ere long;
Else the Puck a **liar** call:
So, good night **unto** you all.

Italian

amends: emenda, ammenda.
break: rompere, rottura, spezzare,
　rompersi, frattura, pausa, schiantare,
　infrangere, sosta, spaccare.
chamber: camera.
fairy: fata.
hare-lip: labbro leporino.
honest: onesto.
idle: ozioso, pigro, folle, inattivo.
issue: pubblicare, emissione,
　problema, emettere, proclamare,
　prole, rilasciare, fascicolo,

discendenza, uscita.
liar: bugiardo.
mark: segno, marcare, marco, marchio,
　contrassegnare, marca, segnare,
　contrassegno, voto.
mole: talpa, molo, neo.
nor: ne.
owner: proprietario, titolare,
　possessore.
palace: palazzo, il palazzo.
pardon: grazia, perdono, perdonare,
　scusare, scusa.

prodigious: prodigioso.
safety: sicurezza.
sweet: dolce, soave, caramella.
unearned: non guadagnato.
unto: a.
weak: debole, fiacco.
yielding: cedendo.

Give me your **hands**, if we be friends,
And Robin shall **restore** amends.

[Exit.]

Italian

hands: mani.
restore: ripristinare, ripristiniamo,
 ripristini, ripristinano, ripristinate,
 ripristina, restaurare, ripristino,
 restaura, restauriamo, restauri.

GLOSSARY

abide: aspettare, aspettiamo, aspetta, aspettano, aspetti, aspetto, aspettate, restare, sopportare
abridgment: compendio
absence: assenza, mancanza
accent: accento, accentare, accentano, accentate, accenti, accentiamo, accenta
according: secondo
ace: asso
acorn: ghianda
acquaintance: conoscenza, conoscente
actor: attore
actors: attori
adder: vipera
address: indirizzo, indirizzare, recapito, discorso, l'indirizzo
adieu: addio
admirable: ammirabile, ammirevole, mirabile
admiring: ammirando, ammirativo
advance: avanzare, anticipo, proporre, avvicinarsi, anticipazione, avanzamento, avanzata, acconto, progredire, prestito, progresso
advances: avanzamenti
advantage: vantaggio, beneficio, guadagno, profitto
affair: affare, faccenda, caso
affection: affetto, affezione, amore
afraid: pauroso, inquieto, spaventato, angoscioso, impaurito
aggravate: aggravare, aggravo, aggrava, aggravano, aggravate, aggravi, aggraviamo, peggiorare
aim: scopo, proposito
air: aria
airy: arioso
alone: solo, da solo, solamente
aloof: appartato, in disparte, alla larga, a distanza, distante
altar: altare
alter: cambiarsi, alterare, altera, alteriamo, alterano, alteri, alterate, altero, modificare, mutare, cambiare
amazed: sbalordito, stupito, si stupito

amen: amen
amend: emendare, emendo, emendiamo, emendi, emendate, emendano, emenda
amends: emenda, ammenda
amiable: amabile
amiss: male, inopportuno
amorous: amoroso
ancient: antico
angel: angelo
anger: collera, rabbia, ira
angry: arrabbiato, irato, stizzito
anguish: angoscia
anoint: ungere
answer: risposta, rispondere, replicare, rispondere a
answers: risposta, risposte
antique: antico
apace: di buon passo
apartment: appartamento
apparel: vestimento, abito
appear: apparire, apparite, appariamo, appari, appaiono, appaio, parere, comparire
appears: appare
apple: mela, la mela
appointed: nominato
apprehend: capiamo, capisci, capisco, capiscono, capite, temono, comprendono, temete, comprendi, afferro, temo
apprehension: apprensione, arresto
approach: accesso, approccio, avvicinare, avvicinamento, avvicinarsi, accostare
apt: adatto
arm: armare, braccio, arma, il braccio, armi
arrow: freccia, saetta
art: arte, l'arte
artificial: artificiale, artefatto
aside: da parte, a parte
ask: chiedere, chiedi, chiediamo, chiedo, chiedete, chiedono, domandare, domando, domandate, domandi, domandiamo
asleep: addormentato

ass: asino, ciuco, somaro, culo
assurance: assicurazione, promessa
assure: assicurare, assicura, assicuriamo, assicurate, assicuri, assicurano, assicuro, garantire
athenian: ateniese
athens: Atene
attend: visitare, curare, assistere, curiamo, curi, curo, curano, visitate, visitiamo, cura, visiti
attendant: custode, compagno, inserviente
attending: visitando, curando, assistendo
attractive: attraente, seducente, allettante, attrattivo, avvenente
audacious: audace
audience: udienza, uditorio, pubblico
aunt: zia, la zia
austerity: austerità
autumn: autunno, l'autunno
avouch: garantire
awake: sveglio, svegliarsi
aye: sì
bachelor: scapolo, celibe, baccelliere
badge: distintivo, badge
bags: borse
bait: esca
balance: equilibrio, saldo, bilancio, bilanciamento, bilanciare, equilibrare, bilancia, quadrare, pareggio
ballad: ballata
bank: banca, banco, la banca, sponda, riva
bankrupt: fallito, bancarotta, fallimento
bare: nudo, denudare
bark: corteccia, abbaiare, scorza, latrare, abbaio
barren: sterile
bashfulness: timidezza
battle: battaglia, combattimento
batty: pazzo
bead: perlina
bear: orso, produrre, ribassista, partorire, l'orso, portare

beard: barba
beards: barbe
beast: bestia, animale
beat: battere, picchiare, sbattere, battimento, battito
beautiful: bello, carino, bella, bellissimo
beauty: bellezza
becomes: diviene, diventa
bed: letto, il letto
beds: letti
befall: succedete, succedi, succediamo, succedo, succedono, succedere
beg: mendicare, mendicano, mendica, mendicate, mendico, mendichiamo, mendichi, chiedere, elemosinare, supplicare
begin: cominciare, cominci, cominciate, cominciano, comincia, cominciamo, comincio, iniziare, inizi, iniziate, iniziano
beginning: inizio, cominciando, principio, iniziando
behold: guardare
bent: curvo, piegato
berries: bacche
beseech: supplicare, scongiurare, implorare
besides: inoltre, d'altronde
betwixt: tra
bid: offerta, offrire, chiedere
bill: conto, fattura, becco, biglietto, cambiale, effetto, tratta, nota, banconota, bolletta, buono
bird: uccello, l'uccello
bitter: amaro
blade: spada, pala, lametta, lama
blameful: biasimevole, riprovevole
blameless: irreprensibile
bless: benedire, benedi', benedite, benedicono, benedico, benedici, benediciamo
blessed: benedetto, beato
blessedness: beatitudine
blink: lampeggiare, ammiccare
bliss: felicità, beatitudine
blood: sangue
bloody: sanguinante, sanguinoso, maledetto, cruento
boar: verro
board: consiglio, asse, tavola, commissione, bordo, scheda, pannello
bog: palude, acquitrino, pantano
boiling: bollente, ebollizione, bollitura, bollire
bold: grassetto, spesso, grosso, audace
bolt: bullone, chiavistello, catenaccio
bond: legame, obbligazione, collegare, vincolo

bones: ossa
bosom: petto, seno
bottle: bottiglia, imbottigliare, la bottiglia
bottom: fondo, basso, carena
bouncing: robusto, rimbalzare, grosso, rimbalzo
bower: ancora di prora, pergolato
boy: ragazzo, servire
brake: freno, frenare
brave: coraggioso, valoroso, strenuo, affrontare
bravely: coraggiosamente
bread: pane, impanare, il pane
break: rompere, rottura, spezzare, rompersi, frattura, pausa, schiantare, infrangere, sosta, spaccare
breast: petto, seno, mammella
breath: alito, respiro, fiato, soffio
breathless: ansante, senza fiato
brief: breve, corto, riassunto, conciso, memoria
bright: brillante, luminoso, splendente, chiaro
bring: portare, portiamo, porti, portano, portate, porto, porta
broke: al verde, rovinato, scarti di fabbricazione
broom: scopa, granata, ginestra, la scopa
brought: portato
brow: sopracciglio, fronte
bud: bocciolo, germoglio, germogliare, gemma
bully: prepotente
bum: scroccare
burr: bava
bury: seppellire, seppelliamo, seppellisci, seppellisco, seppelliscono, seppellite, sotterrare
bush: arbusto, cespuglio, boccola, bussola
busy: occupato, affaccendato, indaffarato
buy: comprare, comperare, acquisto, acquistare, compra
c: ci
calendar: calendario
call: chiamare, chiami, chiamiamo, chiamo, chiamano, chiama, chiamate, chiamata, appello
calls: chiama
candle: candela, la candela, cero
cannot: non potere
capacity: capacità, capienza
carcass: carcassa
carpenter: falegname, carpentiere
carried: portato, trasportato
carries: porta, trasporta
carry: portare, porti, portate, portiamo, portano, porto, porta,

trasportare, trasporta, trasportano, trasportate
carthage: Cartagine
cat: gatto, il gatto
catch: prendere, prendi, prendono, prendete, prendiamo, prendo, fermo, colpire, colpiscono, colpisco, colpiamo
catching: contagioso, prendendo, infettivo, colpendo, prendere
cause: causa, causare, provocare
celestial: celeste, celestiale
chain: catena, catenina
chamber: camera
chance: caso
chaplet: sopporto per anima, ghirlanda
charge: carica, carico, addebito, spese, onere, tassa, caricare, imputazione, accusa
charm: fascino, incanto
charmed: affascinato
chaste: casto
cheek: guancia, la guancia
cheer: rallegrare
cherries: ciliege
cherry: ciliegia
chide: sgrida, sgrido, sgridiamo, sgridi, sgridano, sgridate, sgridare
chiding: sgridando
chief: capo, principale
childhood: infanzia, fanciullezza
chink: fessura
choice: scelta
choose: scegliere, scegli, scegliamo, scegliete, scelgo, scelgono, eleggere, eleggete, eleggi, eleggiamo, eleggo
circumference: circonferenza
civil: civile
clamorous: clamoroso
clean: pulito, pulire, puliamo, pulite, puliscono, pulisco, pulisci, puro, netto, lindo
cloister: chiostro
close: chiudere, vicino, chiudo, chiudono, chiudiamo, chiudete, chiudi, prossimo, chiuso
cobweb: ragnatela
cock: gallo, cazzo, rubinetto
coil: bobina, rotolo
cold: freddo, raffreddore
colour: colore
colt: puledro
comedy: commedia
comes: viene
comfort: consolare, comodità, confortare, comfort, benessere
coming: venendo
commend: lodare, loda, lodiamo, lodo, lodi, lodate, lodano, raccomandare, vantare
commit: commettere

common: comune, volgare, ordinario
companion: compagno, accompagnatore
compare: confrontare, confronta, confrontiamo, confronti, confrontano, confrontate, confronto, paragonare, paragono, paragona, paragonate
compass: bussola, la bussola, compasso
compel: forzare, costringere, forzate, costringete, forzo, forziamo, forzi, costringi, forza, costringono, costringo
comprehends: comprende
con: contro
conceive: concepire, concepiamo, concepisci, concepisco, concepiscono, concepite
concern: riguardare, concernere, cura, azienda, importanza, preoccupazione
conclude: concludere, concludo, concludono, concludiamo, concludi, concludete
conclusion: conclusione, risultato
concord: accordo
confer: conferire, conferiamo, conferisci, conferiscono, conferite, conferisco
conference: conferenza, congresso
confess: confessare, confessa, confessano, confessate, confessi, confessiamo, confesso
confounding: confondendo
confusion: confusione
congealed: congelato
conjunction: congiunzione
conjure: evochiamo, evochi, evoca, evocate, evoco, evocano, fare incantesimi, evocare
conscience: coscienza
consent: consenso, concordare, essere d'accordo, accordo, benestare, assenso, acconsentire
consider: considerare, consideri, considerano, consideriamo, considera, considerate, considero, guardare
consort: consorte, coniuge
content: contenuto, contento, soddisfatto, soddisfare
convenient: conveniente
cool: fresco, raffreddare, freddo
corn: granturco, callo, mais, grano, granoturco, cereale
coronet: corona nobiliare, corona
costs: costo, costi
cottage: casolare, villetta, casetta
counsel: consiglio, avvocato, consigliare, raccomandare, avviso
counterfeit: falso, falsificare

couple: coppia, accoppiare, paio, consorti, coniugi, agganciare
couples: coppia
courageous: coraggioso
courageously: coraggiosamente
course: corso, percorso, piatto, andamento, decorso, direzione, rotta, portata
courteous: cortese
courtesy: cortesia
cover: coprire, coperta, copertura, copertina, percorrere, coperchio, legatura
coward: codardo, vigliacco
cowardice: codardia, vigliaccheria
cowardly: vigliacco, codardo
cowslip: primula
cradle: culla, luogo d'origine, cullare
cranny: fessura, crepa
crawl: strisciare
created: creato
creature: creatura
credit: credito, accreditare, avere
creep: strisciare, strisci, strisciamo, strisciano, strisciate, strisciamento, striscia, striscio
creeping: strisciando, strisciante
creeps: striscia
crescent: mezzaluna
crete: Creta
crew: equipaggio, squadra
crimson: cremisi
crop: raccolto
cross: croce, attraversare, irato, incrociare, incrocio, varcare, valicare, traversare, accavallare
crow: cornacchia, corvo
cruel: crudele
crush: schiacciare, schiacciamento, accasciare, frantumare
cry: piangere, grido, gridare, urlare
cuckoo: cuculo
cue: stecca
cunning: astuzia, astuto, furbo
cupid: cupido
cups: tazza
cur: cagnaccio
curse: bestemmiare, maledire, imprecare, maledizione, imprecazione
curtsy: inchino, riverenza
customary: consueto, usuale, abituale
cut: taglio, tagliare, tagliato, taglia, incisione
dagger: pugnale, daga
dainty: delicato
dale: valle
damned: dannato, maledetto
dance: ballare, ballo, danza
dank: bagnato, umido
dares: osa
dark: scuro, oscuro, buio, oscurità,

tenebroso
darkness: oscurità, tenebre
date: data, dattero, datare, appuntamento
daughter: figlia, figliola, figliuola, la figlia
daylight: luce del giorno
dead: morto
dear: caro, costoso, egregio
debate: dibattito, dibattere, discussione
debt: debito
deceiving: ingannando, truffando, ingannare
deep: profondo, fondo, intenso, cupo
defeated: sconfitto, sconfitta, sconfiggere
delay: ritardo, tardare, ritardare, indugio, indugiare
delight: delizia, deliziare, dilettare, diletto, godimento, rallegrare, gioia
derision: derisione
desert: deserto, abbandonare
deserve: meritare, meritano, merita, meritate, meritiamo, meriti, merito
deserved: meritato
desire: desiderio, desiderare, bramare
despatch: inviare, spedizione
despise: disprezzare, disprezza, disprezzano, disprezzate, disprezzi, disprezziamo, disprezzo
device: dispositivo, apparecchio, congegno
devices: dispositivi
devour: divorare, divorano, divora, divorate, divoriamo, divoro, divori
devoured: divorato
dew: rugiada
dewlap: giogaia
die: morire, muoio, muori, muoiono, morite, moriamo, dado, cubo, matrice, stampo
died: morto
dies: muore
dined: pranzato, cenato
dirty: sporco, sporcare, imbrattare, insudiciare
discharge: scarico, scarica, portata, scaricare
discharged: scaricato
discord: disaccordo
discourse: discorso
discretion: discrezione
disdainful: sdegnoso, sprezzante
disfigure: sfigurare, sfiguriamo, sfiguri, sfiguro, sfigurate, sfigurano, sfigura
disgrace: vergogna, disgrazia, disonorare, disonore
disobedience: disubbidienza
dispose: disporre, disponete, dispongo, dispongono, disponi,

disponiamo
dissembling: dissimulando
distant: distante, lontano
distracted: distratto
disturb: disturbare, disturbiamo,
  disturba, disturbano, disturbate,
  disturbi, disturbo
divine: divino
dog: cane, il cane
dole: sussidio
dotage: rimbambimento
dote: essere rimbambito
double: doppio, sosia, raddoppiare,
  duplice
doubt: dubitare, dubbio
dove: colomba, piccione
downright: completamente, schietto
dragons: draghi
draw: disegnare, disegna,
  disegniamo, disegni, disegnate,
  disegnano, disegno, tirare, attrarre,
  sorteggio, eguaglianza
drawn: disegnato
draws: disegna
dreadful: terribile
dream: sogno, sognare
dried: secco
drink: bere, bevanda, bibita
drop: goccia, diminuire,
  abbassamento, abbassare, caduta
drowned: annegato
drowsy: sonnolento
dry: secco, seccare, asciutto, essiccare,
  asciugare
duchess: duchessa
duck: anatra, anitra, l'anatra
due: dovuto
duke: duca
dulcet: melodioso
dull: opaco, smussato, spuntato
dumb: muto
dumbly: mutamente
dust: polvere, spolverare
duty: dovere, dazio, imposta,
  mansione
ear: orecchio, spiga, l'orecchio,
  pannocchia
earnest: serio, caparra
ears: orecchie
ease: agio, facilità
eastern: orientale
easy: facile, semplice
eat: mangiare, mangi, mangia,
  mangiamo, mangiano, mangiate,
  mangio
echo: eco, echeggiare
edict: editto
eight: otto
elf: elfo
embarked: imbarcato
employ: usare, impiegare, assumere,
  occupare

empty: vuoto, vuotare, vacuo
endure: sopportare, sopporta,
  sopporto, sopportiamo, sopporti,
  sopportano, sopportate, tollerare,
  durare, duriamo, dura
enmity: inimicizia
enrich: arricchire, arricchiscono,
  arricchite, arricchisco, arricchisci,
  arricchiamo
enter: entrare, entra, entrano, entrate,
  entri, entriamo, entro, invio
enthralled: affascinato
entice: attirare
entreat: supplicare
epilogue: epilogo
error: errore, sbaglio, fallo
errs: erra
estate: fattoria, patrimonio, tenuta
esteem: stima, rispetto, stimare,
  considerazione, considerare,
  rispettare, riguardo
etc: ecc
eternally: eternamente
eunuch: eunuco
everlasting: eterno
evermore: sempre
everything: tutto
examine: esaminare, esaminate,
  esamino, esamini, esaminano,
  esamina, esaminiamo
excellent: eccellente, esimio, ottimo
excuse: scusa, scusare,
  giustificazione, pretesto
exile: esiliare, esilio, esule, bandire,
  esiliato
exit: uscita, uscire, l'uscita
exploit: sfruttare, utilizzare, exploit,
  impresa
exposition: esposizione
expound: spiegare
extempore: estemporaneo
eye: occhio, cruna
fade: dissolvenza, svanire, svanisci,
  svanite, svanisco, svaniamo,
  svaniscono, sbiadire, avvizzire,
  appassire
fail: fallire, morire, mancare
faint: debole, svenire, svengo,
  svengono, sveniamo, svenite, svieni,
  svenimento, vago
faintness: debolezza
fair: biondo, fiera, giusto, bazar,
  correttamente, bello, equo
fairly: abbastanza, equamente
fairy: fata
faith: fede, fiducia
faithful: fedele, leale
fall: cadere, caduta, autunno, cadono,
  cado, cadiamo, cadi, cadete,
  diminuire, calo, piombare
fallen: caduto
falling: cadendo

falls: cade
false: falso, finto
fan: ventilatore, ventola, tifoso,
  ventaglio, ammiratore
fancy: figurarsi, capriccio,
  immaginazione
fare: tariffa
farewell: addio, congedo
farther: più lontano
farthest: il più lontano
fashion: moda, modo
fast: veloce, digiuno, velocemente,
  presto, digiunare, rapido
fat: grasso, grosso, pingue, spesso
fate: destino, fato, sorte
fault: difetto, faglia, guasto, fallo
favour: favorire, favore
fawn: cerbiatto
fear: paura, temere, angoscia, timore,
  aver timore
fearful: spaventoso, pauroso
feast: banchetto, festa
feigning: fingendo
fell: abbattere
fellow: uomo
female: femmina, femminile
fetch: portare, portiamo, porto, porti,
  portate, portano, porta, ottenere,
  andare a prendere
field: campo, settore
fierce: feroce
fiery: infuocato
fight: combattere, duellare, lotta,
  lottare, battaglia, picchiarsi,
  combattimento
figs: fichi
figure: figura, calcolare, cifra, numero
filly: puledra
finch: fringuello
finds: fonde, fonda
fine: multa, contravvenzione,
  multare, bello, delicato, carino,
  eccellente, penale, ammenda
finger: dito, il dito
fingers: dito
fire: fuoco, incendio, sparare, rogo
fit: adattare, aggiustare, apoplessia,
  in forma, adatto
fitted: aderente, adatto, attrezzato
fled: fuggito
flies: vola
flood: inondazione, alluvione,
  allagare, alta marea, inondare,
  diluvio, sommergere, allagamento,
  piena
flourish: fiorire, fiorisci, fiorisco,
  fioriscono, fiorite, fioriamo,
  prosperare
flout: schernire
flower: fiore, fiorire
flowers: fiore
flowery: fiorito

flute: flauto, scanalatura
fly: volare, voli, volate, voliamo, vola,
   volo, volano, mosca
foe: nemico
fog: nebbia, annebbiare
fold: piegare, piega, plica, ovile,
   grinza, stabbio
follow: seguire, seguiamo, seguite,
   seguo, seguono, segui
followers: seguito
follows: segue
folly: follia
fond: tenero, affettuoso, affezionato
food: cibo, alimento, generi
   alimentari, vivanda
fool: babbeo, sciocco, allocco,
   ingannare
foolish: sciocco, stupido, stolto,
   ignorante, fesso
force: forza, forzare, costringere,
   vigore
forest: bosco, foresta, selva
forester: guardia forestale,
   guardaboschi
forgot: dimenticato
former: precedente, passato
forms: moduli
forth: avanti
fortnight: due settimane
fortunately: fortunatamente, per
   fortuna
forty: quaranta
forward: avanti, spedire, attaccante,
   in avanti, inoltrare
foul: fallo
fountain: fontana, sorgente, fonte
fourth: quarto, quarta
fowler: uccellatore
fox: volpe, la volpe
fragrant: profumato, fragrante,
   odoroso
frame: telaio, intelaiatura, cornice,
   fotogramma, incorniciare, struttura,
   inquadrare, immagine,
   incastellatura, ordinata
french: francese
frenzy: frenesia
fresh: fresco
fret: agitazione, consumare, greca
friend: amico, amica
friendly: amichevole, cortese,
   amicale, gradevole, benevole,
   carino, grazioso
friends: amici
friendship: amicizia
fright: paura, spavento, timore,
   angoscia
frolic: cattivo
frown: cipiglio
fruitless: infruttuoso, inutile
function: funzione, impiego,
   funzionare, mansione

fury: furia, furore
gait: andatura
gallant: galante, coraggioso, valoroso
gallantly: galantemente
gambol: capriola
game: gioco, giuoco, cacciagione,
   selvaggina, partita
garments: indumenti
garter: giarrettiera
gate: cancello, porta, saracinesca,
   paratoia, uscita
geese: oche
generally: generalmente
gentle: mite, gentile, dolce, delicato
gentleman: signore, galantuomo,
   gentiluomo
gently: delicatamente
gift: regalo, dono, presente,
   donazione, omaggio
girdle: cintura
gives: dà, regala
glad: contento, felice, lieto
glance: occhiata, sguardo
glass: vetro, bicchiere, cristallo
glittering: scintillare, brillio, brillare,
   scintillio
globe: globo, mappamondo, sfera
glory: gloria
god: Dio, iddio
goddess: dea
gods: dei
goes: va
gold: oro, d'oro
golden: dorato, aureo, d'oro
gone: andato
goose: oca, l'oca
governess: istitutrice, governante
grace: grazia
gracious: grazioso
grant: concessione, accordare,
   sovvenzione
grapes: uva
graves: tombe
greater: maggiore
green: verde, acerbo
greet: salutare, saluti, salutiamo,
   salutate, salutano, saluta, saluto
grey: grigio, bigio
grim: torvo, truce
grisly: spiacevole, sgradevole,
   orribile
grossness: grossezza, volgarità,
   grossolanità
ground: suolo, fondo, terra, massa,
   terreno
grove: boschetto
grow: crescere, crescete, crescono,
   cresco, cresci, cresciamo, coltivare,
   coltiviamo, coltivo, coltivi, coltivate
growing: crescendo, coltivando
grown: cresciuto, coltivato
grows: cresce, coltiva

grunt: grugnito, grugnire
guilty: colpevole
habitation: abitazione
hail: grandine, grandinare
hair: capelli, capello, pelo,
   capigliatura
hairy: peloso, capelluto, villoso,
   irsuto
handful: manciata
handicraft: artigianato, mestiere
hands: mani
hang: pendere, appendere,
   sospendere, impiccare
happy: felice, contento, lieto, beato
hard: duro, pesante, difficile, dura,
   solido
hare-lip: labbro leporino
hark: ascoltare
harm: danno, nuocere, danneggiare
harmonious: armonioso, armonico
haste: fretta, furia
hate: odiare, odio, detestare
hated: odiato
hateful: odioso
hatred: odio
haunt: frequentare
haunted: frequentato, perseguitato
hawthorn: biancospino
hay: fieno
headless: senza testa
hear: udire, odono, odi, odo, udite,
   udiamo, sentire, sentono, sento,
   sentite, senti
heard: udito, sentito
hearing: udendo, sentendo, udito,
   udienza, ascolto
heart: cuore, il cuore
hearts: cuori
heat: calore, riscaldare, ardore, caldo,
   scaldare
heaven: cielo, paradiso
heavier: più pesante
heaviness: pesantezza
heavy: pesante, grave
heed: cura, attenzione
height: altezza, altitudine, altura
helen: Elena
hell: inferno
hempen: di canapa
hence: da qui, quindi
henchman: accolito
herb: erba, erbe
hercules: Ercole
herein: qui
hers: suo
hide: nascondere, nascondo,
   nascondiamo, nascondono,
   nascondete, nascondi, pelle,
   nascondersi, pellame, celare,
   occultare
highness: altezza
hill: collina, colle, altura

hinders: impedisce
hither: qui, quà
hoard: ammasso, ammassare
hobgoblin: spiritello maligno
hog: porco, maiale
hold: tenere, stiva, stretta, mantenere, ritenere
holding: tenere, tenuta, detenzione, podere, presa
hole: buco, foro, apertura, forare, buca, bucare
honest: onesto
honey: miele
honour: onore
hope: speranza, sperare, spera, sperano, sperate, speri, speriamo, spero
horned: cornuto
horse: cavallo, il cavallo
hot: caldo, piccante
hound: cane da caccia
hour: ora, l'ora
hours: ore
housewife: casalinga, massaia
howsoever: comunque
hue: tinta
human: umano
humour: umore, umorismo
hundred: cento, centinaio
hung: appeso
hungry: affamato
hunting: cacciando, caccia
hurt: ferire, far male, ferita, dolere
hymn: inno
ice: ghiaccio, glassare
icy: ghiacciato, gelato
idle: ozioso, pigro, folle, inattivo
ill: malato, ammalato
illusion: illusione
imagination: immagine, immaginazione, fantasia
imagine: immaginare, figurarsi, immagino, immaginiamo, immagini, immaginano, immaginate, immagina
imagining: immaginando
imitate: imitare, imitano, imito, imitiamo, imitate, imita, imiti, contraffare
impair: danneggiare, danneggiano, danneggiate, danneggio, danneggi, danneggia, danneggiamo
impaired: danneggiato
impeach: accusi, incrimino, incriminiamo, incrimini, incriminate, incriminano, incrimina, accusiamo, accusate, accusano, accusa
imperfection: imperfezione
imperial: imperiale
impression: impressione, impronta
inconstant: incostante

incorporate: incorporare, includere
increase: aumento, aumentare, ingrandire, incremento, incrementare, accrescere
indeed: davvero, infatti, di fatto, veramente
indian: indiano, indiano americano
injury: ferita, lesione, danno, torto
intend: intendere, intendono, intendo, intendete, intendiamo, intendi
intent: intento, intenzione
interlude: intermezzo, interludio, intervallo
invisible: invisibile
iron: ferro, ferro da stiro, stirare
issue: pubblicare, emissione, problema, emettere, proclamare, prole, rilasciare, fascicolo, discendenza, uscita
ivy: edera
jaws: ganasce
jealous: geloso
jest: scherzare, scherzo
join: congiungere, congiungi, congiungiamo, congiungo, congiungono, congiungete, legare, unirsi, lego, lega, legano
joiner: falegname
jove: Giove
joy: gioia
judgment: giudizio, sentenza
juggler: giocoliere
juice: succo, sugo
keen: aguzzo, acuto, tagliente, affilato
kill: uccidere, ammazzare
killed: ucciso
killing: uccisione
kindred: parentela, affine
king: re
kingdom: regno, reame
kinsman: parente
kiss: bacio, baciare, baciarsi
kissing: baciare
knavery: bricconeria
knavish: furfantesco, da briccone, disonesto
kneel: inginocchiarsi
knight: cavaliere, cavallo
knit: lavorare a maglia, aggrottare
knows: conosce, sa
lack: mancanza, mancare, manchiamo, manchi, mancate, manca, mancano, manco, difetto, carenza
ladies: signore
lady: signora, dama
laid: posato
lamentable: lamentevole, deplorevole
languish: languire
lantern: lanterna

lap: lappare, grembo
lark: allodola
late: tardi, tardo, in ritardo, tardivo
latter: ultimo
laughing: ridere, risata
laughter: risa, risata, riso
lay: posare, posiamo, poso, posi, posate, posano, posa, laico
lazy: pigro, indolente
lead: piombo, condurre, conduciamo, conducono, conduco, conducete, conduci, guidare, guidiamo, guidano, guidate
leaden: di piombo
leads: conduce, guida
league: lega, banda
learning: imparando, apprendimento
least: minimo, meno
leave: lasciare, abbandonare, partire, lasciano, partono, partite, partiamo, parti, lasciate, lasciamo, lascia
led: condotto, guidato
legs: gambe
length: lunghezza, durata
lesser: minore
lest: affinchè non, per paura che
lets: affitta
leviathan: leviatano
liar: bugiardo
lie: mentire, bugia, giacere, menzogna
light: luce, leggero, accendere, chiaro, illuminare, fanale, lampada, luminoso, debole
lighter: accendino, chiatta, bettolina
lightning: fulmine, baleno, lampo
likeness: somiglianza, rassomiglianza
lily: giglio
lime: calce, lime
linen: lino, biancheria
lingers: indugia
lion: leone
liquid: liquido
liquor: liquore
listen: ascoltare, ascolti, ascoltiamo, ascoltate, ascoltano, ascolta, ascolto
live: vivere, vivete, vivono, viviamo, vivi, vivo, abitare, abiti, abita, abitano, abitate
livery: livrea
lives: vive, abita
living: vivendo, abitando, vivo, vivente
loam: argilla
loath: contrario, restio
loathe: detestare, detesti, detesto, detestiamo, detestano, detesta, detestate, avere in orrore
loathed: detestato
loathing: detestando, ripugnanza
longer: oltre, più lungo

looks: guarda
loose: sciolto, lasco, slegare, slacciare, sciogliere
lord: signore
lordship: signoria, dominio
lose: perdere, perdiamo, perdete, perdi, perdo, perdono
lost: perso, perduto, smarrito
loud: forte, alto, rumoroso
loved: benvoluto
lovely: bello, piacevole, amabile, grazioso, gradevole, affascinante, caro, carino
lover: amante
loves: amore
loving: affettuoso
low: basso
lower: inferiore, abbassare, abbassate, abbassi, abbassiamo, abbassano, abbassa, abbasso, calare, abbattere
luck: fortuna
lullaby: ninnananna
lunatic: pazzo, lunatico
lurk: nascondersi
luscious: delizioso, succulento
lying: mentire, bugiardo, giacente
mad: matto, pazzo, arrabbiato, rabbioso, folle
madly: pazzamente, follemente
madman: pazzo
madmen: pazzi
maid: cameriera, ragazza
maiden: nubile, fanciulla
makes: fa, commette
manager: direttore, amministratore, manager, gestore, gerente, dirigente, amministratore delegato
manhood: virilità
manly: virile
manner: maniera, modo
manners: educazione
mantle: mantello, manto
mare: cavalla
mark: segno, marcare, marco, marchio, contrassegnare, marca, segnare, contrassegno, voto
marred: guastato, rovinato, sciupato
married: sposato, si sposato
marry: sposare, sposati, sposatevi, si sposi, si sposate, si sposano, ci sposiamo, mi sposo, maritarsi, ammogliarsi, maritare
marshal: schierare, maresciallo
marvel: meraviglia, stupirsi
marvellous: meraviglioso
mask: maschera, mascherare, mascherina
master: maestro, padrone, principale, master, dominare, anagrafica
match: fiammifero, accoppiare, corrispondenza, partita, cerino
meaning: significato, intenzione,

accezione, senso
meant: significato
meantime: frattanto, nel frattempo, intanto
measure: misura, misurare, provvedimento
meddling: ingerenza
medicine: medicina, medicinale, farmaco
meditation: meditazione
meet: incontrare, incontra, incontriamo, incontri, incontrano, incontrate, incontro, confluire
meeting: incontrando, convegno, riunione, incontro, adunanza, comizio, assemblea
melancholy: malinconia, malinconico
melody: melodia
mercy: misericordia
mermaid: sirena
merry: allegro, festoso, gaio
met: incontrato
middle: mezzo, medio, metà, di mezzo
midnight: mezzanotte
midst: mezzo
mighty: poderoso, forte, possente, potente
mild: mite, dolce
mile: miglio
milk: latte, mungere, il latte
mimic: imitare, mimetico, imitativo
mine: miniera, mina, minare, estrarre
minute: minuto, il minuto, minuscolo, momento
minutes: verbale, contravvenzione, minuti
mirth: gaiezza, allegria, ilarità, gioia
mischief: birichinata
miserable: miserabile, misero, afflitto, cattivo, triste, povero, miserevole, miserando
mistake: errore, sbaglio, sbagliare, confondere, fallo
mistaken: sbagliato
mistress: padrona
mock: deridere, deridono, derido, deridiamo, deridi, deridete, finto, beffare
mockery: derisione
modesty: modestia, verecondia
mole: talpa, molo, neo
momentary: momentaneo
monkey: scimmia, la scimmia
monster: mostro
monstrous: mostruoso
moon: luna, la luna
moonlight: chiaro di luna
moonshine: chiaro di luna
moral: morale
morn: mattino
morrow: domani

mortal: mortale
moth: falena, tarma, tignola
motion: movimento, mozione, moto
moulded: stampati
mountains: montagne
mourning: lutto, piangendo
mouse: topo, sorcio, mouse, il topo
mouth: bocca, imboccatura, foce, la bocca, apertura
move: muovere, muoversi, spostare, mossa, movimento, traslocare, trasportare, trasferire, commuovere
mows: falcia, rasa
muddy: fangoso, torbido
mulberry: gelso
munch: sgranocchia, sgranocchio, sgranocchiate, sgranocchiamo, sgranocchi, sgranocchiano, masticare rumorosamente, sgranocchiare
mural: murale
murder: omicidio, assassinare, assassinio
murderer: assassino
music: musica, la musica
musical: musicale, musical
mutual: reciproco
myself: mi, me stesso, io stesso
nails: chiodi
names: nomi
nativity: natività
natural: naturale
nature: natura, indole, carattere
naught: nulla, zero
nay: anzi
near: vicino, prossimo, presso
nearly: quasi
neck: collo, pomiciare, il collo
needs: necessità, bisogno
negligence: negligenza, trascuratezza, condotta negligente
neigh: nitrire, nitrito
neither: ne, neanche, nemmeno, neppure
neptune: nettuno
news: notizie, novità, notizia
nick: tacca
nightingale: usignolo
nightly: di ogni notte, ogni notte
nimble: agile
nine: nove
noble: nobile, gentilizio, nobiliare
nodding: cenno del capo
noise: rumore, schiamazzo
none: nessuno
nor: ne
notably: notevolmente
note: nota, biglietto, appunto, annotazione, notare, annotare
notwithstanding: nonostante
nuptial: nuziale
nuts: matto

nymph: ninfa
nymphs: ninfa
oak: quercia
oath: giuramento, imprecazione
oaths: giuramenti
oats: avena
obedience: ubbidienza, obbedienza
object: oggetto, cosa, scopo
observance: osservanza
observation: osservazione
odious: odioso
odorous: odoroso
offence: reato, infrazione, offesa, scandalo
offend: offendere, offendiamo, offendo, offendi, offendete, offendono, insultare, insulto, insulti, insultate, insultano
offer: offerta, offrire, proporre, presentare, proposta
offices: uffici
oft: spesso
opportunity: opportunità, occasione
orient: oriente, orientare
original: originale
ought: dovere
ounce: oncia
overcast: coperto
overhear: origlia, origliate, origlio, origli, origliano, origliamo, origliare, udire per caso
owl: gufo, civetta
owner: proprietario, titolare, possessore
ox: bue
pace: passo, andatura, velocità
page: pagina, valletto
pains: dolori
painted: dipinto, verniciato
pairs: pari
palace: palazzo, il palazzo
pale: pallido, smorto, impallidire
pap: pappa
paper: carta, documento, tappezzare, relazione, giornale, la carta
paradise: paradiso
paragon: esemplare
paramour: amante, drudo
pardon: grazia, perdono, perdonare, scusare, scusa
pare: pelare
parents: genitori, i genitori, padre e madre
park: parco, parcheggiare
parting: separazione, divisione
partition: partizione, parete divisoria, tramezzo
partly: in parte, parzialmente
parts: ricambi, parte
pass: passare, passaggio, lasciapassare, passata, trascorrere, passo

passed: passato
passing: passeggero, passare, passaggio
passion: ardore, passione
passionate: appassionato, ardente
pat: colpetto
patched: rappezzato
patches: toppe
patent: brevetto, brevettato, palese, brevettare
paths: percorsi
patience: pazienza
patiently: pazientemente
pause: pausa, sosta
paved: pavimentato
paying: pagando
pays: paga
peace: pace
pearl: perla
peck: beccare
peep: occhieggiare, pigolio, pigolare, sbirciare
perceive: percepire, accorgersi, scorgere, percepiamo, scorgo, scorgiamo, scorgi, scorgete, percepite, scorgono, percepiscono
perchance: forse
perfect: perfetto, perfezionare
perforce: necessariamente
performing: eseguendo
peril: pericolo
perish: perire
perishing: perendo
personage: personaggio
persuasion: persuasione
pert: impertinente
piece: pezzo, parte, porzione
pierce: perforare, perfora, perforo, perforiamo, perfori, perforate, perforano, trapassare
pillow: guanciale, cuscino
pipes: tubi
piping: tubatura
pity: compassione, pietà
plaster: intonaco, intonacare, cerotto, gesso
play: giocare, giocano, giocate, giochiamo, gioca, giochi, gioco, suonare, suona, suoni, suoniamo
played: giocato, suonato
player: giocatore
playfellow: compagno di giochi
playing: giocando, suonando
plays: gioca, suona
plead: peroro, supplico, suppliamo, supplichi, supplicate, supplica, peroriamo, perori, perorano, perora, imploro
please: piacere, per favore, per piacere, prego
pleasure: piacere, gradimento
plot: complotto, trama, macchinare,

complottare, appezzamento, intreccio, congiura, disegnare
ploughman: aratore
pluck: rompere, staccare, cogliere, spennare, strappare, fegato
plunge: tuffarsi, immergere, tuffare, immersione
points: punti, scambio
pomp: pompa, fasto
poor: povero, cattivo
potion: pozione
pour: versare
powers: poteri
praise: lodare, lode, elogiare, encomio, elogio
pray: pregare, pregate, prego, preghi, prega, preghiamo, pregano
prayer: preghiera, orazione
prayers: preghiere
preferred: preferito
premeditated: premeditato
prepare: preparare, prepari, prepariamo, preparate, preparano, prepara, preparo, allestire, allestiamo, allestisci, allestisco
preposterously: assurdamente
presence: presenza
present: presente, regalo, dono, presentare, attuale
presented: presentato
presently: attualmente
press: premere, pressa, torchio, stringere, pressare, serrare, stampa, torchiare, pigiare
pressed: premuto
pretty: grazioso, bellino, carino, bello
primrose: primula
princess: principessa
prison: prigione, carcere
private: privato, senza impiego, riservato
privilege: privilegio, privilegiare
proceed: procedere, procedete, procedono, procedo, procediamo, procedi
prodigious: prodigioso
progeny: progenie
prologue: prologo
promise: promessa, promettere, promettono, promettete, prometti, promettiamo, prometto
proper: decente, proprio
prosecute: perseguire, persegui, perseguiamo, perseguite, perseguo, perseguono, perseguitare
prosperity: prosperità
prospers: prospera
proud: orgoglioso, fiero
prove: provare, proviamo, provi, provate, provano, provo, prova, comprovare, dimostrare
proverb: proverbio

proves: prova
provided: provvisto, fornito
puck: disco
pumps: pompe
puppet: bambola, burattino, marionetta, pupazzo
pure: puro
purge: epurazione, purgare, pulire, purga, spurgo, epurare, eliminare, purgante
purple: viola, porpora, rosso porpora
purpose: scopo, proposito, fine, intenzione
pursue: perseguire, persegui, perseguite, perseguo, perseguiamo, perseguono, perseguitare, inseguire
pursues: persegue
pursuing: perseguendo
pursuit: inseguimento, ricerca
quaint: bizzarro, antiquato
quake: tremito, tremare
queen: regina
quell: soffocare, soffochi, soffochiamo, soffocate, soffocano, soffoca, soffoco
quick: rapido, svelto, veloce
quickly: presto, rapidamente, velocemente
quiet: calmare, tranquillo, placare, quieto, calmo, zitto, silenzioso, quiete
quill: penna d'oca
quince: mela cotogna, cotogna
radiant: radiante, raggiante
rage: furore, ira, furia, collera
raging: furente, infuriato, furioso
rail: rotaia, parapetto, guida
rain: pioggia, piovere, la pioggia
rare: raro, al sangue
rarely: raramente
rash: eruzione, avventato, eruzione cutanea
raven: corvo, corvo imperiale, corvino
reach: arrivare, portata, raggiungere, pervenire, estendersi
ready: pronto, disposto
rear: posteriore, retroguardia, retro
reason: ragione, causa, intelletto, ragionare, argomentare, motivo
reasonable: ragionevole, sensato
rebuke: biasimare, disapprovare, riprendere, sgridare, rimproverare
recorder: registratore, flauto dolce
recount: narrare, raccontare
recover: ricuperare, ricupera, ricuperi, ricuperiamo, ricuperano, ricuperate, ricupero, recuperare, guarire, riprendere
recreant: codardo
red: rosso
refuse: rifiutare, rifiutarsi, rifiuti

region: regione, zona
rehearsal: prova
rehearse: proviamo, provo, provi, provate, provano, provare, prova
release: liberare, rilasciare, rilascio, disinnesto, liberazione, svincolo, versione
remain: rimanere, rimangono, rimani, rimango, rimanete, rimaniamo, restare, restiamo, resti, restate, restano
remedy: rimedio, medicina, rimediare
remember: ricordare, ricordiamo, ricorda, ricordano, ricordate, ricordi, ricordo
remembrance: rimembranza, ricordo, memoria
remote: distante, lontano, remoto, isolato, a distanza, periferico
removed: tolto, asportato, rimosso
render: rendere, rendono, rendete, rendi, rendiamo, rendo
renowned: rinomato, famoso
rent: affitto, affittare, canone, noleggiare, pigione
repent: pentirsi
reply: risposta, rispondere, replicare, replica
represented: rappresentato, figurato
request: richiesta, richiedere, chiedere, domanda
respect: rispettare, rispetto, stima
rest: riposo, riposarsi, riposare, resto, pausa
restore: ripristinare, ripristiniamo, ripristini, ripristinano, ripristinate, ripristina, restaurare, ripristino, restaura, restauriamo, restauri
return: ritorno, ritornare, restituire, rientro, contraccambiare, resa, rendere, rivenire, restituzione
revenge: vendetta
revenue: reddito, entrata, ricavi
rheumatic: reumatico
rich: ricco
rid: sbarazzare
rings: anelli
riot: sommossa, tumulto, rivolta, tumultuare
ripe: maturo
rite: rito
rival: rivale
river: fiume
roar: ruggire, muggire, ruggito, scrosciare
roasted: arrostito
robin: pettirosso
rock: roccia, masso, cullare, dondolare, ondeggiare
rod: barra, verga, bacchetta, asta
roll: rullo, panino, rotolare, rotolo,

rullio, rollio, cilindrare
rose: rosa
rotted: marcito
rough: rude, brusco, ruvido, crudo, approssimativo, rozzo, grossolano, scabro, grezzo
royal: reale
rude: scortese, rozzo, maleducato
runaway: fuggiasco
running: correndo, funzionamento, scorrendo, corsa, marcia, corrente
runs: corre, scorre
rush: affrettarsi, giunco, furia
sad: triste, afflitto
safety: sicurezza
sail: vela, veleggiare, la vela, salpare, navigare
saint: santo
sake: causa
salt: sale, salare, salato, il sale
sampler: campionatore
sat: seduto, covato
satire: satira
saucy: impertinente, sfacciato
saying: dicendo, detto, proverbio
scandal: scandalo, maldicenza
scare: spaventare, impaurire, spavento
scene: scena
schooling: istruzione
scorn: disprezzo, disprezzare
scratch: graffiare, graffio, grattare, raschiare, graffiatura, scalfire, unghiata
scroll: rotolo di pergamena, scorrere
sea: mare
seal: foca, sigillo, la foca, sigillare
seat: posto, sede, sedile, seggio, sedia
seeing: vedendo, segando
seek: cercare, cercano, cerchiamo, cercate, cerchi, cerco, cerca
seem: parere, paiono, paiamo, pari, paio, parete, sembrare, sembra, sembrano, sembrate, sembri
seeming: parendo, sembrando, sembrare
sees: vede, sega
seething: bollendo, ribollendo
senseless: insensato
sensible: sensato, ragionevole, sensibile
sent: mandato, spedito
sentinel: sentinella
separation: separazione, distacco
serpent: serpente
servant: servire, servo, servitore
serve: servire, serviamo, servi, servono, servite, servo
setting: regolazione
seven: sette
sex: sesso
shadow: ombra

shady: ombreggiato
shake: scuotere, scuotono, scuoto, scuotiamo, scuoti, scuotete, scossa
shame: vergogna, pudore
shape: forma, formare, figura, foggia, modellare, sagoma
shaping: sagomatura
sharp: affilato, aguzzo, acuto, tagliente, appuntito, piccante, giusto, giustamente, aspro, diesis, nitido
shears: forbici, cesoia
shed: baracca, versare, versate, verso, versiamo, versato, versano, versa, versi, capannone, tettoia
shield: scudo, riparo, proteggere, schermo, schermare
shifting: spostare, spostamento
shine: risplendere, brillare, lustro, splendere
shining: lucente, brillante
shiver: tremare, brivido, rabbrividire
shivering: rabbrividire
shoes: scarpe
short: corto, breve, basso
shot: sparato, sparo, tiro, colpo, scatto
shout: gridare, grido, urlo, sbraitare, urlare
shows: mostra
shrewd: scaltro, sagace, perspicace, accorto
shriek: strillo, strillare
shun: evitare, eviti, evitiamo, evitano, evita, evitate, evito
sick: malato, ammalato
sickness: malattia
siege: assedio
sight: vista, aspetto, avvistare, aria, apparenza
signify: significare, significate, significo, significhi, significa, significhiamo, significano
silence: silenzio
silently: silenziosamente
silver: argento
simple: semplice
simpleness: semplicità
simplicity: semplicità
simply: semplicemente
sing: cantare, canta, cantano, cantate, canti, cantiamo, canto
singer: cantante
single: singolo, celibe, nubile, solo, single
sir: signore
sister: sorella, la sorella
sit: sedere, sediamo, siedono, siedi, sedete, siedo, covare, covo, covi, cova, covate
sitting: sedendo, covando, seduta
skill: abilità, destrezza, maestria
skip: salto, saltellare

slain: ucciso, ammazzato
slay: uccidere, uccidete, uccidono, uccido, uccidiamo, uccidi, ammazzare, ammazza, ammazzo, ammazziamo, ammazzi
sleek: lisciare, lucido
sleep: sonno, dormire, dormi, dormiamo, dormite, dormo, dormono
sleeping: dormendo, addormentato
sleeps: dorme
sleeves: manicotti
slight: leggero, lieve
slip: scivolare, slittamento, sottoveste, slittare, frana, ingobbio
slow: lento
smiling: sorridere
smooth: liscio, piano, levigare, spianare, lisciare
snail: chiocciola, lumaca
snake: serpente
snout: muso, sigaretta, grifo, grugno
snuff: tabacco da fiuto
snug: accogliente, comodo, raccolto
soft: dolce, molle, soffice, morbido, tenero
son: figlio, figliolo, il figlio
song: canzone, canto
soon: fra poco, presto
sorrow: tristezza, cordoglio
sorting: smistamento, cernita, classificazione, ordinamento
soul: anima
sound: suono, sonare, suonare, solido, sondare, sano, scandagliare, rumore, sonda
sovereignty: sovranità
spare: risparmiare, scorta
sparrow: passero
spartan: spartano
speak: parlare, parla, parlo, parliamo, parli, parlate, parlano, favellare
speaks: parla
speech: discorso, orazione, parola
speed: velocità, andatura, rapidità
spell: compitare, sillabare, incantesimo, sortilegio
spend: spendere, spendiamo, spendo, spendi, spendete, spendono, passare, passo, passiamo, passi, passate
sphere: sfera
spirit: spirito, anima
spite: dispetto
spleen: milza, malumore
spoke: raggio
spoken: parlato
sport: sport
sports: sport, sportivo
spotted: maculato
spread: diffondere, spargere, diffusione, spalmare, propagare,

scarto
spring: molla, sorgente, primavera, fonte, saltare, la primavera
spurn: rifiutare, ripulsa, rifiuto
spy: spiare, spia
square: quadrato, piazza, quadro, squadra
squash: schiacciare, zucca
stage: palcoscenico, fase, stadio, scena, palco
stained: macchiato
stamp: francobollo, bollo, bollare, timbro, affrancare, timbrare
stand: stare in piedi, granaio, alzarsi, bancarella
starlight: luce stellare, luce delle stelle
starry: stellato
stars: spighe
starve: affamare
stay: stare, sta', stanno, sto, state, stiamo, stai, restare, rimanere, soggiorno, resta
steal: rubare
stealth: azione furtiva
steel: acciaio, osso di balena, acciaiare, d'acciaio
steep: ripido, erto, scosceso
stern: poppa, severo
stick: bastone, appiccicare, bastoncino, attaccare, incollare, ficcare, bacchetta
stir: mescolare, agitare, muovere
stirring: mescolare, eccitante, agitazione
stomach: stomaco, ventre
stone: pietra, calcolo, sasso, la pietra, ciottolo
stool: sgabello, feci
stop: fermare, ferma, fermarsi, fermo, fermi, fermate, fermano, fermiamo, fermata, cessare, cesso
story: storia, piano, racconto
straight: diritto, destro, dritto, direttamente
strange: strano
stranger: sconosciuto, estraneo, forestiero
streak: stria, striscia
strength: forza, resistenza, robustezza, potenza
strike: picchiare, colpire, battere, sciopero, scioperare, fare sciopero
strong: forte, robusto
stubborn: ostinato, testardo, cocciuto, caparbio
stuff: materiale, farcire, roba, imbottire
sucking: aspirante, succhiare
suffer: soffrire, soffri, soffro, soffrono, soffrite, soffriamo, patire, subire, patiamo, patite, patiscono

summer: estate, l'estate
sun: sole
sunny: soleggiato, assolato
supposed: supposto
sure: certo, sicuro
surgeon: chirurgo
sway: oscillare, ondeggiare, barcollare, oscillazione
swear: giurare, giura, giuro, giuriamo, giuri, giurano, giurate, bestemmiare, imprecare
sweat: sudare, sudore, traspirare
sweep: spazzare, scopare, spazzata
sweet: dolce, soave, caramella
swell: gonfiare, dilatare, rigonfiamento, mare lungo, crescendo
swift: rondone, veloce, rapido, celere
swim: nuotare, nuoto, nuotiamo, nuoti, nuotate, nuota, nuotano, nuotata
swimming: nuotando, nuoto
swoon: svenire, deliquio, svenimento
sword: spada
sympathy: compassione
tailor: sarto
takes: prende
tale: racconto, storia, novella, favola
talk: parlare, parlo, parliamo, parli, parlate, parlano, parla, discorso, discorrere, conversazione, conversare
tall: alto, grande, elevato
tame: addomesticare, domestico, domare
tangled: aggrovigliato
tarry: rimanere, catramoso, rimangono, rimani, rimango, rimanete, rimaniamo
tarrying: rimanendo
tartar: tartaro
task: compito, lavoro, incarico
taste: gustare, gusto, assaggiare, sapore
taunted: schernito, rinfacciato
taurus: Toro
tawny: fulvo
teach: insegnare, insegna, insegnano, insegniamo, insegni, insegnate, insegno, istruire
tear: strappo, lagrima, strappare, lacerare, lacrima
tears: lacrime
tedious: noioso, tedioso
telling: dicendo, raccontando, narrando
tempest: tempesta
temple: tempia, tempio
tempting: allettante, tentando
tend: tendere, prendersi cura di, tendete, tendi, tendiamo, tendo, tendono

tender: tenero, dolce, offerta, tender
tends: tende
terms: condizioni
terribly: terribilmente
testy: stizzoso, irritabile
thank: ringraziare, ringraziano, ringraziate, ringraziamo, ringrazia, ringrazi, ringrazio
thanks: grazie, ringrazia
thee: te
theirs: loro
thence: di là
therein: in ciò
thief: ladro, ladra
thin: magro, sottile
thine: le tue, la tua, i tuoi, il tuo
thinks: pensa
thistle: cardo
thither: là
thorough: completo, accurato
thou: tu
thousand: mille
thread: filo, filetto, filettatura
threats: minaccia
thrice: tre volte
thunder: tuono, tuonare
thy: tuo
thyme: timo
tickle: stimolare, stuzzicare, solleticare, solletico
tide: marea
till: finchè, coltivare, cassa, fino, arare
tipsy: alticcio
tire: gomma, pneumatico, stancarsi, stancare
title: titolo
tomb: tomba, sepolcro
tomorrow: domani
tongs: pinzette
tongue: lingua, linguetta, la lingua
top: cima
topples: crolla, rovescia
torment: tormento
torn: strappato, lacero
torturing: torturare
touch: toccare, tocco, tatto
touching: commovente
toward: verso, a
town: città
trace: traccia, tracciare, delimitare
tragedy: tragedia
tragical: tragico
train: treno, addestrare, il treno, ammaestrare, educare
transformed: trasformato
translated: tradotto
transported: trasportato
transpose: trasporre
tread: pedata, passo, battistrada
treats: leccornie
tremble: tremare
trial: prova, esperimento

trim: rifilare
triple: triplo
triumph: vittoria, trionfo
triumphant: trionfante
true: vero
truly: davvero, infatti, veramente
trust: fiducia, trust, confidenza, affidamento
trusty: fedele, fidato
truth: verità
turf: tappeto erboso, zolla erbosa
turn: girare, giro, svoltare, gira, giriamo, giri, girate, girano, svolta, rovesciare, svoltiamo
turned: girato, svoltato, cambiato
turns: gira, svolta, cambia
tyrant: tiranno
ugly: brutto
undergo: subire, subisci, subisco, subiscono, subite, subiamo
understand: capire, capite, capiamo, capisci, capisco, capiscono, comprendere, comprendono, comprendo, comprendiamo, comprendete
undertake: intraprendere, intraprendete, intraprendono, intraprendo, intraprendi, intraprendiamo
unearned: non guadagnato
uneven: irregolare, ineguale
unfolds: spiega
ungrateful: ingrato
union: unione, sindacato
unkind: brusco, rude, scortese
unknown: sconosciuto, ignoto
unseen: inosservato
unto: a
upbraid: rimproverare, rimprovera, rimproverano, rimproverate, rimproveri, rimproveriamo, rimprovero
usual: usuale, consueto, solito, generale, abituale
utter: totale, completo, proferire, emettere
v: v
valley: valle, vallata
valour: valore
vanishes: sparisce
vantage: vantaggio
vast: vasto
vein: vena
venus: Venere
vexation: irritazione
vile: abietto
villain: furfante
violet: viola, violetta
virgin: vergine
virginity: verginità
virtue: virtù
virtuous: virtuoso

visage: viso, volto
vision: visione, vista
vixen: megera
vow: voto
voyage: viaggio
waggish: scherzoso
wait: aspettare, aspetto, aspetta, aspettano, aspettate, aspetti, aspettiamo, attesa
wake: svegliare, scia, destare
waking: svegliare
walk: camminare, cammino, cammina, camminano, camminate, cammini, camminiamo, camminata, passeggiare, passeggiata
walks: cammina
wall: muro, parete
wander: vagare, vago, errare, vaghiamo, vaga, vagano, vaghi, vagate, vagabondare
wanderer: vagabondo
wandering: vagando, peregrinazione
wane: declinare, declino, declina, declinano, declinate, declini, decliniamo
wanes: declina
wanting: volendo
wanton: sfrenato, scatenato, licenzioso
wants: vuole
warning: avvertendo, avviso, avvertimento, diffida, avvertenza
warrior: guerriero
washes: lava
waste: spreco, rifiuto, scarto, sprecare, sperperare, rifiuti, sprechi, sprechiamo, sprecate, sprecano, spreca
wasted: sprecato
watch: orologio, guardare, sorvegliare, guardia, sentinella, osservare
watery: acquoso
waxen: cereo
ways: modi
weak: debole, fiacco
weapons: armi
wear: portare, usura, logoramento, indossare
weary: stanco, stancare, fiacco
weaver: tessitore
wed: sposarsi, sposare, ci sposiamo, sposati, sposatevi, si sposi, si sposate, mi sposo, si sposano
wedded: sposato
weep: piangere, piangete, piangi, piangiamo, piangono, piango, lacrimare
weeps: piange
weigh: pesare, peso, pesiamo, pesi, pesate, pesa, pesano
welcome: benvenuto, bene arrivate,

accoglienza, gradito, accogliere
western: occidentale
wheat: frumento, grano
wherefore: perchè
whip: frusta, frustare, sferza, sbattere
whisper: sussurrare, bisbigliare, bisbiglio
whistling: fischiare
whit: briciolo
whither: dove
whom: chi, cui
whose: di chi, il cui
wicked: cattivo, malvagio
wide: largo, vasto, ampio
widow: vedova
wife: moglie, la moglie
wild: selvaggio, feroce, selvatico
wilful: intenzionale, testardo
wilt: appassire, appassisco, appassiscono, appassisci, appassiamo, appassite
wind: vento, flatulenza, avvolgere
window: finestra, sportello, finestrino, la finestra
wings: diritti d'acquisto di titoli negoziabili del Governo
winter: inverno, l'inverno
wise: saggio, assennato
wish: desiderio, volere, desiderare, volontà, voglia
wit: arguzia
withdraw: ritirare, ritiro, ritira, ritiriamo, ritiri, ritirate, ritirano, prelevare, ritirarsi, preleva, prelevano
withered: appassito
withering: avvizzimento, appassendo
withholds: trattiene
wolf: lupo
womb: utero, grembo
won: vinto
wonder: stupirsi, stupore, meraviglia, domandarsi, meravigliarsi
wondrous: meraviglioso
wont: avvezzo, abitudine
wonted: usuale, consueto, solito
wood: legno, bosco, selva, legna
woodbine: caprifoglio
word: parola, vocabolo, termine, verbo, formulare
worm: verme, vite senza fine, lombrico, baco
wormy: bacato
worn: consumato, usato, esausto, portato, logoro
worse: peggiore, peggio
worst: peggiore
worth: valore
worthy: degno, meritevole
wrap: avvolgere
wren: scricciolo
wretch: sciagurato

writ: documento, mandato
write: scrivere, scrivi, scrivono, scriviamo, scrivete, scrivo
written: scritto
ye: voi, tu
yellow: giallo
yield: cedere, cedete, cedi, cediamo, cedo, cedono, resa, rendimento, prodotto, fruttare
yielding: cedendo
yields: cede
yoke: giogo, aggiogare
yon: laggiù, là, li
yonder: là, laggiù
yours: il vostro, vostro
yourself: ti
yourselves: voi stessi
youth: gioventù, giovinezza, adolescenza, giovane